RENEWING OUR MINDS IN LOVE

*Integrating Neuroscience and Scripture
for Wholeness and Healing*

Tina J. Smith

Renown
PUBLISHING
WRITE YOUR BOOK & REDEEM CULTURE

Renown Publishing
www.renownpublishing.com

Renewing Our Minds in Love / Tina J. Smith
ISBN-13: 978-1-960236-04-3

Praise for *Renewing Our Minds in Love* by Tina J. Smith

Raised in a religious Evangelical environment I knew what sin was. Lying, smoking and red nail polish were sure to send you to hell. Visiting a therapist was the final nail in your spiritual coffin. I was taught often that mental illness was fiction inspired by the devil. Yet as the Lord revived the inner healing movement through spiritual giants such as Agnes Sanford, our perspectives began to shift.

We needed more than a miraculous touch from God in our bodies. We desperately needed it in our souls. And so the struggle began. How could we marry the wealth of spiritual wisdom to the study of psychotherapy?

It's an honor to walk alongside Tina Smith as she introduces us to a new wave of Christian mental health. Her bold statement, "Neuroscience and Scripture are Integrated" leads you on a journey of self-discovery. If you would allow it, the pages in this book will unlock the secrets to your trauma and the solution to its pain.

I commend Tina for her courage to present such a treasure to the Church. Every counselor will find her practical techniques easy to follow. If you're on the fence regarding the place of Christian therapy in the Church, then this book is what you're looking for.

Apostle Colette Toach
Minister, Author, and Podcaster
ToachMinistries.com
https://www.charismapodcastnetwork.com/show/nextgenprophets

In *Renewing Our Minds in Love*, Tina presents an excellent case for the integration of neuroscience and the truth of God's Word in our personal journey of emotional and mental wellness. Sharing principles learned from science, Scripture, and her own story, she highlights the key elements of love, relationship, and vulnerability that all play a part in our healing story. This is a powerful invitation to partner with Jesus, our true self, and a caring professional to experience authentic healing. If you are seeking your own mental wellness, or leading others toward the same, start reading today and let the transformation begin!

Jeffrey A. Johnston
Lead Pastor of Calvary Assembly in Cambridge, Ontario

It didn't take long to realize, when I became a full-time Christian minister, that if I was going to help people change for good, I needed more than simple biblical principles. Twenty-five years ago, this book would have saved Colette and me many years of discovery.

God created man, which means there are natural and spiritual understandings that need to blend. This book bridges that gap, and helps solve the mysteries, to complete everlasting healing.

...If you are reading this, you mean business. You've just added another powerful tool to your tool belt, which means people will be set free because of your commitment. We need more like you!

Craig Toach
Toach Ministries International
Apostolic Movement International

This book presents fascinating subject matter. As a Christ-follower, pastor, and teacher, [I find] this research has challenged my understanding of the interconnectedness of biblical truth and neuroscience. If you desire to help people on their journey of healing, then Tina's research, insights, and biblical application will be a game changer for you. The content of this book will assist you to help yourself and others find the full freedom that Christ died and rose for humanity to enjoy.

Tim Crooks
Lead Pastor of My Church Winnipeg

This book is dedicated to all my clients, who came with vulnerability and courage. You have been my greatest teachers.

CONTENTS

Introduction   V

PART A: Integration—Neuroscience and Scripture Are Integrated   1

The Capacity to Heal   1

Love or Fear   17

PART B: Wholeness—Holistic Mental Health   27

Interwoven: Spirit, Soul, and Body   29

Led by the Spirit   49

A Model of Care   65

PART C: Limitations—How Religion Limits and Imprisons People   85

The Unbalanced Church   87

Relationship Before Advice   107

PART D: Peace, Freedom, and Love— What Healing Looks Like   121

Freedom in the Eye of the Storm   123

Are You a Free or Shackled Leader?   135

Love Is Foundational   153

About the Author   167

About Renown Publishing   169

Notes   171

Introduction

I was sitting in my clinical office in 2010, posing a question to God about why change is not sustainable. For years, I would discharge clients only to see them return with the same areas of wounding, patterns, and relationship conflicts. My heart hurt for people, as I wanted to see the captives set free.

The Lord began to show me that human beings have a complex design, so change cannot always be narrowed down to altering people's cognitions and telling them to pray or read their Bible more. I remember clearly that my spirit felt heavy for people, because I felt that we were missing something significant.

It was then that I began to gain deeper knowledge and wisdom about what it means to suffer in one's spirit, soul, and body. I hoped that this would lead me to an understanding of how to help people heal and be set free.

I recall sitting in my SUV on lunch break during a training

for mental health practitioners. We were learning about how unresolved traumatic and negative events remain stored in our central nervous system (CNS), ready to activate a flight, fight, or freeze response at the sign of perceived or real danger. People with more complex unresolved trauma may respond with disassociation. Our brains and nervous systems have a powerful ability to help us survive, but not always in healthy and functional ways. We have an impressive messaging system that responds to real or perceived danger through the activation of fear.

As a result of years of wonder, curiosity, and questions, the Lord brought me to the body of research known as neuroscience. The more I learn, the more amazed I am at the intricate design of the human spirit, soul, and body. My journey of discovery has led me to the understanding that *science glorifies God*. Now I want to invite you to journey with me through the marvels of neuroscience, integrated with the word of God.

PART A:
Integration—Neuroscience and Scripture Are Integrated

CHAPTER ONE

The Capacity to Heal

I am convinced that the Bible and neuroscience complement one another and are crucial for understanding how to help people. As counsellors, our goal is to help people heal, grow, and change, yet Christian leaders often overlook the tool God has given us to change: the brain. Pastors and counsellors surely remind people to think, read, and meditate, but that does not address critical realities of neuroscience that have been proven through countless scientific studies.

Unfortunately, there has been a misconception that science and the Bible cannot be integrated into a greater awareness of the soul (the mind and emotions), which has resulted in opposition from both the scientific community and the Christian community. However, I believe that science and the Bible are in complete harmony with one another. I hope that as you read this book, you will see how we can help people by bringing these two disciplines—Bible study or Christian spirituality and neuroscience—together. In short, neuroscience and Scripture are compatible and should be integrated.

BUILDING UPON A BIBLICAL FOUNDATION

As Christians, we are often taught to use the Bible as our exclusive source for discovering the origins of creation and understanding God, His work of salvation, and the intricacies of people's souls and behaviours. We spend countless hours deepening our awareness through biblical training and study. We can access great works from theologians who have studied the Bible word by word and can provide us with a deeper understanding of God's plans, character, and attributes, as well as the reality of the human condition.

The Bible and theology should be our foundation. However, for those who are suffering and broken-hearted, God's mercy may bring healing through the integration of developments in various other disciplines, as long as they are consistent with His word. An integrated approach of this kind can lead people back to the Bible without tactics of shame, judgement, or condemnation.

Wouldn't Christians benefit from resources that provide proof that the word of God is true and substantiated by evidence? Not many Christians would argue that we should ignore historical writings about Babylon or Caesar in order to understand the world and words of the Bible. In the same way, we should not ignore significant advances in neuroscience that help us to understand the world of the soul and enhance our understanding of the Bible. Science glorifies God because it confirms many truths of Scripture.

THE IMPORTANCE OF THE BRAIN AND NEUROSCIENCE FOR THERAPY

Let's consider a different framework of thought that may encourage Christians to reconsider the notion that science and the Bible must remain separate rather than be integrative and supportive. The scientific community has expansive areas of knowledge and research, and it would be too overwhelming to discuss all of them in one book, so I will focus on neuroscience, the study of the brain.

Other than the skin, the brain is the most complex and largest organ of the human body, weighing about three pounds. Researchers state that we "know very little about the brain."[1] This organ controls the body's functions and takes in information from the environment through one hundred billion neurons that communicate in hundreds of trillions of synapsis connections.[2] We can experience the brain's complex functions in the world when we see the fruit of a person's creativity, emotions, intelligence, and memories.

NEUROPLASTICITY AND REWIRING THE BRAIN

For decades, neuroscientists believed that the brain was a non-renewable organ, meaning that brain cells were limited and would slowly die as we age. The hypothesis was that our

3

brains could not change and we were stuck with neuron connections, for better or worse.

However, in 1948, the term *neuroplasticity* was first used by Polish neuroscientist Jerzy Konorski to describe observed changes in the structure of neurons, which are cells that make up our brains. The idea of neuroplasticity goes back even further[3] to when Santiago Ramón y Cajal, the "father of neuroscience," talked about "neuronal plasticity" in the early 1900s.[4] He recognized that, in contrast to current belief at that time, brains could indeed change during adulthood. Cajal asserted, in his words, "a profound belief in the sovereign will; faith in work; the conviction that a persevering and deliberate effort is capable of moulding and organizing everything, from the muscle to the brain, making up the deficiencies of nature and even overcoming the mischances of character—the most difficult thing in life."[5]

In the 1960s, neuroscientists discovered that neurons could reorganize after a traumatic event. As the research continued to develop, it revealed that stress could change the function and the structure of the brain itself.[6] This observed neuroplasticity is the brain's ability to adapt and change. As Dr. Celeste Campbell writes, "It refers to the physiological changes in the brain that happen as the result of our interactions with our environment. From the time the brain begins to develop in utero until the day we die, the connections among the cells in our brains reorganize in response to our changing needs. This dynamic process allows us to learn from and adapt to different experiences."[7]

In other words, the brain is not static but "plastic," or

pliable. Countless MRIs have confirmed that the brain can change in dramatic ways. For example, MRIs from before and after treatment of those with PTSD show that the brain "lights up" differently in scans, indicating the restorative effects of treatment.[8] Our brains can reform and become healthier when we develop healthy thought patterns, self-talk, spiritual disciplines, and relationships. This plasticity has staggering implications for counsellors and therapists who want to help their clients overcome trauma, tragedies, and tribulations.

The fact that we have the capacity to change our brains has profound implications for science *and* for spiritual transformation and discipleship. Many people believe that they are stuck with a particular diagnosis, medication, or habit for life, but the truth is that we can change many of these things as we learn how to change our brains.

FIRE TOGETHER, WIRE TOGETHER

Neuroscientists often say, "When two neurons fire together, they wire together." This axiom was coined by Dr. Donald Hebb, a Canadian neuropsychologist, and it "reminds us that every experience, thought, feeling, and physical sensation triggers thousands of neurons, which form a neural network. When you repeat an experience over and over, the brain learns to trigger the same neurons each time."[9] This means that if our neurons have been wired together at the time of a negative or traumatic experience, we can actually take those neurons and rewire them into a healthier

5

connection.

The human brain is not comparable to any other structure in existence. This organ can update, form different pathways, discard unused pathways, and reorganize based upon our experiences with each other and in the world. In the past, some neurologists thought that we could not change various connections in the brain. However, our knowledge of neuroplasticity has since created breakthroughs in the world of rewiring our brain, which has led to expansive research in the treatment and healing of mental illness.

Instead of believing the lie that we are worthless or must live with shame based on our past experiences and choices, we now know that physical components in our brains can be rewired, leading to improvements in our mental and spiritual health. Discovering that we can rewire our brains to create adaptive and resourceful connections is monumentally profound, as I hope to unpack in the coming chapters.

THE MIND AND THE BRAIN ARE DISTINCT

Contrary to popular belief, the mind and the brain are not the same thing. Dr. Carolyn Leaf, a communication pathologist and cognitive neuroscientist who has researched the mind-brain connection, the nature of mental health, and the formation of memory for almost forty years, has confirmed that the mind is distinct from the brain. The mind has to do with our thoughts, emotions, senses, choices, and experiences. The mind informs the brain so that what is taken in, whether negative or positive, will produce either healthy synapse connections or toxicity in the brain. The latter can lead to mental illness and physical diseases. Dr. Leaf states, "[Your] mind is how you think, feel, [and] choose, and [your] brain is the physical, and they work together to produce what you [do] as a functioning human in society."[10]

The mind is the soul while the brain is the physical organ through which the mind works (much more on this later). Our experiences of life are converted into positive or negative thoughts. The trillions and trillions of thoughts held in experiences and beliefs are nurtured and lead to a wiring of the brain toward fear-based patterns or life-giving patterns. In this way, science confirms that renewing our minds and capturing our thoughts (Romans 12:2; 2 Corinthians 10:5) lead to real and lasting transformation.

THE NONCONSCIOUS AND CONSCIOUS MIND

Dr. Leaf goes on to explain that the nonconscious mind and the conscious mind operate at the same time. The nonconscious mind is the largest part of our existence. The mind receives sound waves, so we think, feel, and choose as our minds process these sound waves. The sound waves are pushed through the brain. The brain responds electromagnetically, chemically, and genetically, activating the growth of proteins and little branches in the brain called dendrites.

Sadly, our world is inundated with chaos, conflict, and trauma, exposing our brains to overwhelming experiences of pain and suffering. How do we fill our minds with and meditate on things that are good and true when our world is filled with fear-based messages around every corner? When our minds attend to the messages found in this world, our brains formulate protective structures out of fear. Scripture tells us that we must set our minds on things above rather than dwelling on the things of this world: "Since, then, you have been raised with Christ, set your hearts on things above, where Christ is, seated at the right hand of God. Set your minds on things above, not on earthly things" (Colossians 3:1–2).

NEUROSCIENCE COMPLEMENTS AND CONFIRMS THE BIBLE

Neuroplasticity may appear to represent only the scientific perspective, but let's consider how this research can reinforce the truth found in the word of God. We read in Romans 12:2, "And do not be conformed to this world [any longer with its superficial values and customs], but be transformed and progressively changed [as you mature spiritually] by the renewing of your mind [focusing on godly values and ethical attitudes], so that you may prove [for yourselves] what the will of God is, that which is good and acceptable and perfect [in His plan and purpose for you]" (AMP).

The Apostle Paul encouraged Christians to renew their minds about two thousand years ago, and science is only recently catching up to this idea. Through rigorous research studies, it has been confirmed that the human brain has been designed to rewire itself and create neuron connections and patterns when we intentionally seek to rewire our brains in a positive manner. We can see in MRIs that the actual substance of the brain changes as people's minds are renewed with Scripture and loving relationships.

The Bible states in 1 Corinthians 2:16, "'Who has known the mind of the Lord so as to instruct him?' But we have the mind of Christ." While we obviously do not know everything that Christ knows, this verse is encouraging us to cultivate Christlike thoughts.

The Scriptures describe our minds as having the ability to choose, through the filtering of information, our thoughts and emotions in order to transform our brains. Paul explained, "We demolish arguments and every pretension that sets itself up against the knowledge of God, and we take captive every thought to make it obedient to Christ" (2 Corinthians 10:5). Are we aware of our thoughts and intentionally filtering them, or do we allow our responses and self-talk to reign free? When we take our thoughts captive and use discernment to filter through them, we are engaging in the process of renewing our minds. We must be intentional and diligent about this.

PATHWAYS TO RENEWING OUR MINDS

The Bible says that our minds and lives can change as we continue to think about good, noble, and pure things, and neuroscience confirms this biblical truth.

Finally, believers, whatever is true, whatever is honorable and worthy of respect, whatever is right and confirmed by

9

God's word, whatever is pure and wholesome, whatever is lovely and brings peace, whatever is admirable and of good repute; if there is any excellence, if there is anything worthy of praise, think continually on these things [center your mind on them, and implant them in your heart]. The things which you have learned and received and heard and seen in me, practice these things [in daily life], and the God [who is the source] of peace and well-being will be with you.
—**Philippians 4:8–9** *(AMP)*

When we expose our five senses to good and pure things, our brains change. When I read the word of God, my mind receives it, which then changes the mechanisms and matter in my brain. Neuroscience has shown us that, as the Bible says, the mind can change as we renew our thoughts and form positive behavioural habits.

THE IMPORTANCE OF RELATIONSHIPS

Many Christians find that although they memorize Scripture, worship on Sundays, and attend Bible studies, they still do not experience the change they desire. This is often because a relational component is missing. We cannot experience transformation outside of relationships.

First, our relationship with God must be dynamic so that we are not merely going through the motions of worship and reading the Bible, but rather have a heartfelt, vibrant connection to God. People can recite Bible verses over and over again in a religious manner without having a healthy relationship with their Father in heaven. Countless studies show that people have a deep need for love and relationships, which mirrors God's triune (relational) nature and confirms all that He says about loving Him, loving our neighbours, and the need for the church community to be rooted in love.

WIRED TO LOVE OR TO FEAR

In addition to a close, personal relationship with God, we must cultivate healthy relationships with people for transformation to take place. This is why people go to see therapists. Most of what therapists do is relationship-based, and clients often feel that they do not receive enough help in this area from their busy pastors or fellow Bible-study attendees. Much of what I do is centered on building a relational foundation so that people have the freedom to open up, which is necessary for healing.

Attachment determines how our brains are wired. Our relationship with our parents can determine how our brains form. If children have secure and safe relationships with their caregivers, their brains will wire in a healthy manner. If not, the neurons may wire in an unhealthy way. Research shows that brains can be wired to love or to fear.[11] The more the amygdala in the brain is activated, which creates the fight, flight, or freeze response, the more the person is motivated by fear and living in survival mode. Exposure to trauma, abuse, or detached parenting can result in the brain wiring itself in a fearful manner, leading to mental illness or physical diseases. This is why loving relationships are so critical for mental health.[12]

Designed in Love and for Love

We often hear that children are resilient. This is not true! Children are only resilient when they have been equipped by loving adults (parents or other caregivers) with the resources that make them resilient.

In Kathy Brous's painful story of healing, *Don't Try This Alone,* she quoted John Townsend: "In the absence of relationship, we experience condemnation [and a] good deal of negative, critical self-talk."[13] Her story of healing reveals that we are not meant to heal deep wounds of abandonment and rejection alone, but through safe, secure, and loving relationships.

For this reason, the conventional wisdom that children are born resilient is misguided. Resilience is developed over time through love-based relationships, which lead to brains that are wired in a loving manner. Without this, children may develop safety mechanisms that can ultimately sabotage their relationships as part of an unconscious survival strategy.

When the brain and the nervous system have been activated negatively, they work together to develop a plan to create safety. Exposure to fear or trauma leads to unhealthy patterns in the brain that are not easy to undo. The preface of *Don't Try This Alone* states that "when an infant instead experiences excess stress or lack of response from adults, its instincts read that as a survival threat. This floods the baby with fight-flight stress chemicals like cortisol."[14] When a child's brain is wired in a negative way, it will hinder the formation of healthy relationships. It is as if the child puts on armour to protect herself, but this armour also imprisons her.

On the other hand, exposure to love leads to a healthier brain. This is an exciting discovery in the field of neuroscience because it confirms another scriptural principle: people are made in the image of God (Genesis 1:26–28). Since God is love (1 John 4:7–21), it makes sense that human beings, as God's image-bearers, need love to function properly.

NO LOVE, NO CHANGE

People cannot change if they do not feel worthy of changing. This is why relationships are so crucial. A loving relationship helps the person seeking counsel to feel known and cared for. In this context, change can occur. The critical ingredient for transformation from a neurological perspective, the tangible experience of helping people, comes down to how intentional the leader is in forging a healthy, loving relationship with those in need.

Telling a parishioner to do more, pray more, read more, or attend church services and Bible studies more does not lead to lasting change. It usually leads to the person feeling guilty for not measuring up. Instead, relationships need to be built so that trust is established. Changes in the mind and brain that lead to lasting transformation are planted in the soil of these loving relationships.

This is why the Bible calls us to practice the "one anothers." We are to "love one another" (John 13:34), "instruct one another" (Romans 15:14), "be patient, bearing with one another in love" (Ephesians 4:2), "be kind and compassionate to one another, forgiving each other" (Ephesians 4:32), "encourage one another" and "build each other up" (1 Thessalonians 4:18; 5:11), "live in harmony with one another" (Romans 12:16; 1 Thessalonians 5:13), "offer hospitality to one another" (1 Peter 4:9), "carry each other's burdens" (Galatians 6:2), "rejoice with those who rejoice; mourn with those who mourn" (Romans 12:15), and comfort one another (2 Corinthians 1:3–4).

When we know that God is love (1 John 4) and that He gave His Son for our salvation (John 3:16), we can experience His transforming love, especially in fellowship with other Christians. This may be one reason why Jesus said that the greatest commandments are to love God and to "love your neighbor as yourself" (Matthew 22:37–39). He said that the whole Old Testament could be summed up in these two commandments (Matthew 22:40). Without the foundation of love, personal and spiritual growth is stunted.

HOW CHANGE OCCURS

Pastors have complained to me that their congregants come to them repeatedly with the same story or problem. One pastor asked me, "Why don't they just change? Why do they keep doing the same thing over and over again for years? I encourage them to pray, read the Bible, and join a small group, but they don't experience the transformation they need."

People do not change, because they do not know how to

alter something that is stored in their brains as a coping mechanism. Out of fear and a desire to survive, the brain is continuing unhealthy patterns that need to change for lives to change. This is why integrating neuroscience with the Christian faith is so critical. Leaders are ignoring the need for the brain to be rewired, or they lack the tools to facilitate this type of change.

The body of Christ needs to understand that God has made human beings in His image and designed us with the capacity to heal through the rewiring of our brains. As you will discover in more depth in the following chapters, this positive change is all based on the foundation of a relational approach, rooted in love, so that we can meet people where they are and engage their spirits, souls, and bodies, including their brains.

Chapter One Notes

_____

_____

_____

_____

_____

_____

_____

_____

_____

_____

_____

_____

_____

_____

_____

_____

_____

_____

_____

_____

_____

_____

CHAPTER TWO

Love or Fear

Neuroscience has shown that our brains become wired to fear or to love. Fear and love cannot exist in the same space in our brains. Scripture tells us, "There is no fear in love. But perfect love drives out fear, because fear has to do with punishment. The one who fears is not made perfect in love" (1 John 4:18).

Human beings have been created by God to love. Love is inherent to our human nature, but fear is not: "For God did not give us a spirit of timidity or cowardice or fear, but [He has given us a spirit] of power and of love and of sound judgment and personal discipline [abilities that result in a calm, well-balanced mind and self-control]" (2 Timothy 1:7 AMP).

God did not design us to fear. He created us to love and to be loved. A survival instinct (which is good) is not the same as a negative, fear-based neuropathway. The latter can lead to an irrational or illogical fear, such as thinking that all relationships are harmful after experiencing a negative one.

FEAR LEADS TO ISOLATION

Our environment, our relationships, and this fallen world can create situations that produce fear in us, leading to a survival response to withdraw and isolate ourselves. Many of these patterns are developed during childhood and may lead us to withhold ourselves from others or, without realizing it, to reject or abandon others to help ourselves feel safe. A brain that becomes wired to fear responds in survival mode almost all of the time. We then develop protective walls and barriers and push people away. In a sense, fear imprisons us.

This fear-based neuropathway is so powerful that it can be passed from a pregnant mother to her developing child. We now know that when a pregnant woman experiences trauma and her nervous system operates in a hyperaroused state, the baby developing in the womb also experiences some of the mom's fear or trauma.[15] Without healing, the mother and child may continue in a cycle of fear, overprotection, and isolation.

Our perceptions can be rooted in a fear-based desire to insulate ourselves. We then perceive feedback at work as being highly critical and worth arguing over rather than helpful, or we set up walls and reduce our ability to receive love from others. This fear-based wiring that stems from past hurt can also determine how we perceive God.

People can usually get over the trauma caused by an earthquake or a tornado in a relatively short amount of time, but they cannot easily or quickly get over the devastation caused by being in a relationship with someone who was supposed to love them and instead harmed them. Their brains become wired according to a fear-based experience because a caregiver was shown to be untrustworthy.

THE ANTIDOTE TO FEAR

On the contrary, a healthy mind is full of love and peace. Scripture says, "You will keep in perfect peace those whose minds are steadfast, because they trust in you" (Isaiah 26:3). Our minds transform our brains when we trust in the Lord and put our hope in His word. As we renew our minds in God's word and take negative thoughts captive, our brains create new connections and synapse responses.

Since God is love, He is the antidote to fear. His love frees us from fear. But the more we are hurt in our lives, the more we will fear and continue pushing people away. This hamstrings the healing process because we need to be in relationships to experience the antidote to fear, which is love.

The antidote to fear is not being told that you are loved, but actually experiencing love. The Bible tells us to put love into action: "Dear children, let us not love with words or speech but with actions and in truth" (1 John 3:18). In order to help people change their fear-based wiring, you must show them that you care for them and love them as they are, thus reflecting God's love.

Counsellors are, in this way, conduits of God's love. It is this love that can lead to peace, because an attribute of love is peace. When we understand that we are fully known and loved by our heavenly Father, we can be at peace. If we live in this peace, we will be free from fear. When we are fully known and loved, we want to change and grow, because we are rooted in grace, not in shame.

MY STORY

When I was thirteen years old, I met a young man in my church's youth group. Because he came from a Christian family, I assumed that he was a healthy young man. I was blinded to the red flags in this boy, as I desired to be seen and loved. That last part was most important: I wanted to be loved.

Sadly, he was abusive toward me during our eight years together. I lived in fear and agreed to marry him, most likely because I was in survival mode. Driving in the car with my parents to the church where I first met him, I leaned over to my bridesmaid and whispered, "I cannot do this." It was a cry for help. However, she was unaware of the pain I was experiencing, so she simply responded, "It is too late."

Two years later, he became more abusive, and I divorced him. I had wrongly assumed that if someone professes to believe in Jesus, that person must know how to love and treat others in a Christlike way. But people can believe in Jesus and not yet be healed of past wounds, or they may only be making a nominal profession of faith.

As you can imagine, after living in an abusive relationship for over a decade, I had put up many barriers in my life and needed time to heal. I eventually remarried, but I focused on protecting myself rather than cultivating a healthy marriage. My brain was wired to survive and push others away, which led me to misperceive my new husband's words and actions during the first five years of our marriage. This can lead to a cycle of dysfunction that is difficult to break, especially if we do not seek help and support.

I was still in survival mode, pushing my husband away. This caused him to feel rejected, which, in turn, stifled any growth toward a healthy, loving relationship. But once I apprehended God's love and experienced His grace in my life, I was able to cast aside those barriers and accept my husband's love. I saw my husband's words and actions in a new light. I was able to love him with God's love flowing through me, and he no longer felt rejected.

"Perfect love drives out fear" (1 John 4:18), but we cannot receive perfect love from sinful human beings. Perfect love comes only from Jesus Christ. Once we experience Jesus' love, we can see people through the lens of His love for others. In fact, it is when we realize that we cannot expect perfect love from fallen people that we can love them and experience their flawed love. We can do this because we have already experienced perfect love from God and do not need it from other people.

At this point, we will not feel inadequate if someone does not love us perfectly or if we fail to love as we should. We also realize that everyone brings his or her own wounds from the past into relationships. If we are rooted and grounded in God's love, then loving ourselves, loving others, and receiving love can be seen and experienced in a new light. Our expectations of others change once we know the source of true and eternal love.

If I expect my husband to love me perfectly, I am creating a codependent relationship with him or turning him into an idol. I am not supposed to be fully dependent on my husband; I am supposed to depend fully on Jesus. I should not seek from man what only God can give.

We often create idols to cover up our wounds. If I am feeling anxious, rather than turning to God, I might start doing some online shopping. Or, if my parents failed to love me, I might expect my husband to love me perfectly and heal me, something that only God can do. In this case, I would have created an idol out of my husband and placed a burden upon him that he could not bear. An idol cannot love or heal us; only Christ can.

FULLY KNOWN AND LOVED

When we read the Bible, we often see Jesus sitting and eating with hurt and broken people, outcasts in society, such as prostitutes and despised tax collectors. (Tax collectors were considered traitors because they collected taxes for the Romans, who were occupying Israel. They often lined their pockets with inflated rates that drained poor people of their hard-earned money.) Jesus would sit with children face-to-face rather than standing over them.

I try my best to think of those passages when someone walks into my office, seeking help. That is, I try hard never to think, *"How can I change you?"* Instead, I think, *"How can I get to know you? Tell me who you are. I want you to be fully known and fully loved."* I seek to model my love for people after Jesus' unconditional love.

My goal is to look people in the eyes and let them know that they are seen and heard. This helps them to experience love, which is needed for healing. When people know that someone genuinely cares for them and is not trying to change them, they are free to move forward.

THE CATALYST FOR TRANSFORMATION

This love and acceptance leads people to the door of vulnerability, which can show them the path to transformation. The Bible exhorts us, "Accept one another, then, just as Christ accepted you, in order to bring praise to God" (Romans 15:7). People do not change because someone tells them to change. People change when they know that they are loved as they are. Then they are willing to make the changes that someone who loves them suggests, because there is trust in the relationship. Without this acceptance, it is difficult for people to be vulnerable, gain self-awareness, and grow in their relationship with God.

Unfortunately, more times than not, people are being told that they are loved in the church, but they are not experiencing love. They feel condemned or criticized, because they are being told to do more, try harder, or be holier, without a foundation of genuine love. It may be that they are not engaged in close relationships with people from the church or that the message they hear from the pulpit lacks grace.

When people seek counsel in the church, they often feel that the pastor wants to fix them, not truly know them. The cycle of fear and mistrust continues, and no genuine experience of love or transformation occurs. On the other hand, when we truly love people with God's love that is flowing through us, they will feel known and accepted and be ready to embrace the change they have been seeking.

Chapter Two Notes

Part B:
Wholeness—Holistic Mental Health

CHAPTER THREE

Interwoven: Spirit, Soul, and Body

"Are you praying enough? Are you reading the Bible every day? Are you memorizing Scripture? Are you spending enough time with the Lord?" For many of my clients who attend various denominations within the body of Christ, these questions have produced more harm than good and have led to defeatism and condemnation. While pastors mean well when they encourage spiritual disciplines, they have often misdiagnosed the problem and, therefore, are prescribing the wrong medicine.

"DO MORE AND TRY HARDER"

Countless clients have sat on my couch and said that a person in leadership made them feel like they were not doing enough spiritually, so their faith must be weak. The advice to "do more and try harder" is often misinformed and misguided. Many of my clients have asked me, "Tina, I spend

29

every day with the Lord, praying and reading His word, so why am I not better?" Church leadership has wrongly led people to believe that if they pray and read more, all will be well. Has neglecting various aspects of what it means to be human contributed to this error?

Soon after hearing pastoral instructions to try harder, people begin to believe that God views them through the grid of a checklist. Maybe they see God as Santa Claus, with his "naughty or nice" list. They start to view a relationship with God as being based on their works rather than God's grace and the finished work of Christ. This perspective leads people to question their faith or relocate to a new church, where they hope to find answers but instead are left with the same experience.

We need to see and address problems through a new lens. It is not the truth we are changing; it is our approach. Some churches are so focused on the law or truth that there is little emphasis on a relationship with Christ and relationships with other people. Other churches are so focused on relationships that they are devoid of truth or they water it down.

People were drawn to Jesus, who called Himself "the truth" (John 14:6), because He was loving. He never compromised the truth for the sake of love or love for the sake of truth. He always upheld both. Our approach must take biblical truth reinforced by neuroscience into account and express it through love.

"NEVER GOOD ENOUGH"

Over the years, I have met many people who said that they left the church because they never felt good enough or that they had done enough. Others believed that God had forsaken them since they could not keep up with the church-imposed demands of spiritual disciplines. Some people ultimately decided to walk away from a God who seemed not to care about them.

All Christians, including church leadership, are called to experience the journey of becoming Christlike, as expressed in the nine fruits of the Holy Spirit: "love, joy, peace, forbearance, kindness, goodness, faithfulness, gentleness and self-control" (Galatians 5:22–23). These fruits do not grow in isolation, but rather in relationships. The fruits of the Holy Spirit are birthed and developed as we walk with other people, even when they cause us to be frustrated or confused. While spiritual disciplines are essential, it may be the case that someone in your church needs a good friend more than the memorization of another Bible verse.

SHAPED BY OUR GAZE

Our heavenly Father's will is to mold us every day, and His mercies are "new every morning" (Lamentations 3:22–23). Our Abba, our Father, reaches inside our very souls and draws our attention to Him. The Scriptures tell us that if we have seen the Son, we have seen the Father (John 14:9). If we focus on Jesus instead of ourselves, we will be shaped into His image (2 Corinthians 3:18).

God's greatest gift to us is His relentless mercy. Oxford defines *mercy* as "compassion or forgiveness shown toward someone whom it is within one's power to punish or harm."[16] If people are not grounded in God's grace, love, and mercy, they will find their identity in their practice rather than in their unchanging position in Christ.

MERCY IN ACTION

The challenge for every Christian is to make this mercy tangible in the lives of the broken-hearted by accessing greater wisdom and knowledge rather than relying on one-dimensional approaches. The assumption that someone who is struggling is "not doing enough" cannot be applied to all people in all situations at all times. We must depart from this cookie-cutter method if we are truly to help people find their way to the transformative work of the cross. We need a multidimensional approach.

CONFLICTED ABOUT COUNSELLING

I remember feeling conflicted one morning regarding the recurrent message from church leadership that seeing a counsellor was ungodly, even if the counsellor was a Christian. We were told that Christians should see only their church leadership for support and that psychology was worldly.

My heart was broken for those who had stepped out of their church, often away from messages of shame and condemnation they were receiving there, to seek counselling and hope. People sat on my couch, overwhelmed by guilt and feeling conflicted over this teaching. They could not access "shame-free" help at the church and were feeling guilty for pursuing it outside of the church.

I was saddened and confused by this perspective and the lack of support from churches, which are supposed to reflect the mercy that God has extended to all of us. I spent time with the Lord, asking Him, "Is it wrong for people to see a Christian counsellor?" I sat for a long time, praying and crying out to the Lord, as I sought His will for me and my clients. I could not comprehend the belief that seeking a Christian counsellor who walks in wisdom, is relational, and seeks knowledge that leads people to Jesus could be wrong. This was the first time I had ever questioned my perspective on this matter.

PLANS SUCCEED WITH COUNSELLORS

It was then that the Lord said in my spirit, "Tina, I give people Christian counsellors like you out of My mercy and My compassion for the hurting and the broken." He then took me to a scripture in the book of Proverbs that states, "The wise will hear and increase their learning, and the person of understanding will acquire wise counsel and the skill [to steer his course wisely and lead others to the truth]" (Proverbs 1:5 AMP).

In God's mercies, which are fresh every morning through

33

His steadfast love for us, He gives us wise counsellors to walk with us through our struggles. Proverbs 11:14, 15:22, and 20:18 also encourage us to seek counsel.

Why would a gracious God ever limit our ability to access healing that would glorify Him, especially through gifted counsellors? Granted, not all secular psychology aligns with God's word, but I have found that many therapies complement the Scriptures.

I have been practicing in mental health since 1998, and I have always wondered why pastors have seen people as merely spiritual beings while neglecting the needs of the soul and the body. Christians tend to minimize God's creation of the body and consider only spiritual ideas. However, Paul stated that we are "spirit, soul and body" (1 Thessalonians 5:23). The prayer in that verse for the "whole spirit, soul and body" to "be kept blameless at the coming of our Lord Jesus Christ" infers that parts of our tripartite being can be impaired if we are not careful to keep all of them blameless.

INTEGRATING VARIOUS DISCIPLINES

Oftentimes our struggle has to do with trauma in the body and not a lack of faith. Some counsellors basically say, "Just believe you're not worthless, and then you'll feel better." This approach does not address deeper issues beyond the mind. If you transform your mind, it can change your spiritual life. But for many people, the information in their bodies deters them from accepting new beliefs. Sometimes we must start with healing the body before the soul can heal.

For example, I came across a treatment method called Eye Movement Desensitization and Reprocessing (EMDR) and became trained and certified in it. This experiential therapy replicates REM sleep and helps the brain to "digest" painful memories.

As I began to use this method with clients, I saw God heal many people of past trauma. People who had tried everything else said that through EMDR, they were finally set free from their past. Some people have said that they felt like Jesus was holding them through this process, or they heard a choir of angels. Others felt like the Holy Spirit was removing the wax from their ears that had prevented them from hearing God's voice.

I tell my colleagues that we must become the best historians of our clients' lives because history causes present-day impact. We have to go backward to move forward, or else our past can hold us hostage. Going back to the past does not mean that the cross has not redeemed us. Rather, we are still bearing the stain of sin from our past that requires Holy Spirit sanctification.

ADDRESS THE WHOLE PERSON

How does this knowledge impact our ability to help support people outside of a one-dimensional framework? When we see people as more than spiritual beings, we learn to meet others exactly where they are without sharing messages of blame and shame, such as "you are not doing enough."

The body of Christ needs to access greater knowledge of

how the spirit, soul, and body can impact our ability to heal and to walk in freedom. The Bible tells us to be led by the Holy Spirit, which means that there must be a spiritual priority. However, we also have an enemy who prowls about (1 Peter 5:8), looking "to steal and kill and destroy" (John 10:10) the plans God has for us, and this enemy impacts our souls and bodies.

The world is filled with stories of destruction, suffering, and sorrow that leave the soul and the body heavy with negativity and trauma. The Bible tells us that we will face trials and tribulations, but God has not left or forsaken us (John 16:33; Deuteronomy 31:6; Hebrews 13:5). How do you tell someone's soul and body this biblical truth when that person is carrying the weight of the world and the deception of the enemy has set up a stronghold? When the person seeking solace in a church family is told, "You are not doing enough," it further compounds the enemy's lies. Now this person believes that he or she is not good enough, perhaps even worthless.

EMPHASIZE LOVE AND RELATIONSHIPS

How do we change to a more helpful approach? We need to understand what true help looks like within the context of relationships. There must be congruence of words and behaviours, with an emphasis on love. When church leadership or congregants say, "You are loved," they should follow this declaration with actual demonstrations of that love, such as a check-in or an invitation to be heard over dinner or in a meeting.

Brené Brown, an American research professor, lecturer, author, and registered social worker, spent ten years of her career studying vulnerability, courage, worthiness, and shame. In her book *The Gifts of Imperfection: Let Go of Who You Think You're Supposed to Be and Embrace Who You Are*, she explains: [17]

> We cultivate love when we allow our most vulnerable and powerful selves to be deeply seen and known, and when we honor the spiritual connection that grows from that offering with trust, respect, kindness, and affection.
>
> ...Shame, blame, disrespect, betrayal, and the withholding of affection damage the roots from which love grows. Love can only survive these injuries if they are acknowledged, healed, and rare.

Hurting people need to know that they have not been forgotten or rejected. Loving relationships are foundational to helping people access healing. A relationship built on "compassion, kindness, humility, gentleness and patience" (Colossians 3:12) ensures the foundation of trust and vulnerability that dismantles walls of pain held in the spirit, soul, and body.

SHARE THE STORIES IN OUR SOULS

We will not feel welcomed in the life of another if we cannot set the stage for healing ourselves. We must show up for ourselves in our own healing journey before we can do this well with another person.

Our experience of the healing process occurs when someone else hears the stories held in our souls and felt in our bodies. Through dialogue, we come to understand the complexities of our stories that we cannot heal by simply praying more or reading the Bible more. By God's grace, He will look upon the faces of His children, meet us exactly where we are, and enable true healing. Then He will use us as vessels of His love in the lives of the broken-hearted.

I have been given the most incredible privilege and blessings to be invited into the lives of many people. It is a gift when people are vulnerable with me because they know that they are in a safe place with no judgement. I witness their tears as they share stories of experiences that have caused them to question their faith or question God's existence.

Sometimes when people are sharing their stories with me, their nervous systems are twisted so tightly that their bodies ache, their breathing is shallow, and their hearts race. I see the pain on their faces that speaks without words. There are profound stories held in the non-verbal expressions of posture and visual cues that often go unseen. These visual cues are a window that creates an opportunity to engage with people who are hurting and feel like no one understands them. As we spend more time caring for God's children, we will learn to interpret the expressions of the body that say more than words.

Listen Outside the Prison Door

People are filled with anguish due to perceptions in their minds resulting from wounds others have given them. It feels like living in a prison to which Satan has the keys. They need someone to show up who is willing to sit outside the prison door and get to know them, not someone who tries to force the door open with empty words or religious talk devoid of love. This person who sits outside the prison door hears the story of the soul, sees the pain held in the body, and understands that the spirit is wounded with doubt, disbelief, and loss.

God, in His mercy, calls the broken-hearted out of their prisons. He sends willing vessels of His love to sit outside the prison door faithfully and continually until the prisoner's spirit receives comfort and begins to take back authority. A compassionate, kind, and patient person is a salve to the soul. The intentionally and mindfully present helper can observe and engage the interwoven suffering held within the spirit, soul, and body.

Exhausted from Trying It All

Over the years of working with Christians and non-Christians, I have seen how similar suffering presents itself in every client. The desperation to be seen, heard, validated, and loved through relationships is ubiquitous. It is the common denominator expressed by all people who feel this inner void as a result of their past and present experiences.

After testing whether our relationship was built on trust and a non-judgemental attitude, Christians have declared on the couch, "Tina, I have tried it all. I've tried deliverance sessions, inner-healing sessions, praying, and reading my Bible for hours a day. But nothing is changing." They are left with the painful belief that something is wrong with them and they will never be okay.

Non-Christians have expressed, "I have tried everything from new-age treatments to medications to meditative practices, and the list goes on."

The emptiness is still clearly present though their secular world view does not allow them to understand the complexities of the soul and body. Whether Christian or non-Christian, we keep trying the same methods over and over again, hoping that they will, at some point, overcome the condition of humanity.

I have seen how the spirit, soul, and body are intertwined in suffering. The body that hurts tells the soul, "I can't do this anymore." The soul tells the body, "Just stay in bed longer. You're always going to be in pain, so what's the point in trying?" The spirit, entrenched in religious duty, lags behind as though it were the tail and not the head (Deuteronomy 28:13). However, the Lord provides us with another way to live through the leading of the Holy Spirit, who empowers us to take back our authority rather than letting our souls and bodies weave messages of harm.

For both Christians and non-Christians, suffering begins in the soul and body and then affects the spirit. Entrenched suffering produces a shell or shield that prevents Christians from hearing the voice of the Holy Spirit and following His leading. The pain held in their souls and bodies muffles the sound of that "still small voice" (1 Kings 19:12 NKJV) and impairs their ability to become whole.

Non-Christians live in the same condition, but they do not know the One who saves; they only hear about the character of Jesus from the supposedly (from their perspective) divine book called the Bible. The suffering held in the souls and bodies of non-Christians hardens their hearts and prevents them from perceiving the truth of the gospel message.

Love, when expressed through a willing and intentional vessel, activates the ability to gain insight, healing, and wholeness. It is foundational to leading people to healing and the cross of Jesus Christ. We will not have the privilege of gaining insight into how the spirit, soul, and body are interwoven, both in suffering and in healing, if we are not willing to sit outside the prison door long enough for others to choose to let us in. If we are unable to be present, open, non-judgemental listeners, it reveals something concealed in our own spirits, souls, and bodies that is not surrendering in humility to the call to help the broken-hearted. We must experience the "refiner's fire" (Malachi 3:2) or enter into a season in the wilderness, as the Israelites did, without staying longer than we are called to stay.

THE INTERWOVEN NATURE

Dr. Caroline Leaf describes the spiritual portion of our tripartite design as our spirit being, our intuition, and the part of us that communes with God.[18] The soul is the mind, made up of our intellect, emotions, and will. The body includes our physical form and all of its components, such as the brain and other organs and the central nervous system.

The body, including the brain, is led by the will of the soul, and the soul is designed to be led by the spirit. Furthermore, God calls us to be led by the Holy Spirit and to commune in worship with our heavenly Father. We read in Psalm 143:10, "Teach me to do your will, for you are my God; may your good Spirit lead me on level ground." Romans 8:14 tells us that "those who are led by the Spirit of God are the children of God."

The interwoven nature comes into play when the soul influences how the body experiences joy and suffering, and vice versa. For example, the soul, which is influenced by freewill thinking, may believe, "I am not good enough," which then causes a heaviness and an ache in the body. This experience can show up as increased heart rate, shallow breathing, or nausea. The perception of oneself held in the mind creates a corresponding emotional and physical experience, which invariably impacts the person's ability to hear from the Holy Spirit.

I want you to imagine being in session with an individual who has just discovered that she was sexually abused as a child and feels shame and guilt every time her husband wants to connect intimately. Her body has a strong reaction when he wants to connect with her. She wants to avoid affection with her husband due to the trauma held in her body.

The results of her historical experience of sexual abuse have never been repaired, so her brain comes up with a plan to flee by disengaging with her husband or giving in but feeling frozen and robotic. When she wants to say "no," it causes her husband to feel strong emotions of rejection. They both begin the cycle of believing something defective about themselves, such as "I am not good enough" or "I am worthless." The physical trauma from the past is like cancer in the body that spreads easily to the soul and the spirit and continues causing damage.

The alert system in the brain, which is attached to the hippocampus, sends messages down the central nervous system as it remembers a negative event. The hippocampus holds the sensory information of unresolved memories. It activates the amygdala, which sends messages down the central nervous system to activate a strategy, such as fight or flight.

The wife's body alerts her to the danger of being touched as her body remembers past abuse. The husband's central nervous system felt this sensation before, when he was a boy and his mom rejected and abandoned him. Both the husband and the wife have experiences held in their brains and nervous systems that alert them to the danger zone.

This cyclical relationship pattern clouds their perceptions and remains unresolved because it often happens subconsciously. The body holds memories even if the mind does not consciously think about them. The overarching spiritual reality is that Satan speaks through the mind and continues to affirm the lies that the wife and the husband believe.

The interwoven nature of the spirit, soul, and body begins with experiences in the environment that wire the brain to fear. "The body holds the final score," as Bessel van der Kolk writes in one of his books.[19] The body holds the truth of one's experiences from the past. We can try to convince ourselves logically that something is not a big deal, but our bodies will still reveal significant indicators if something is not right.

THE BODY MUST BE ADDRESSED

The brain becomes wired to internalized beliefs about oneself associated with thoughts of unworthiness, inadequacy, and being unlovable, insignificant, or responsible for another person's actions. This recurring pattern of internalizing beliefs wires the brain to funnel only information that supports these beliefs, thus recycling the process. This leaves the brain to focus on somatic responses that have been emotionally, physically, and psychologically unsafe in order to create a plan of safety, even though these defense mechanisms are often unhealthy.

The alarm system continues to be activated as the brain loses its ability to sort information factually. The perceptions are strengthened, and the body engages with a flight, fight, or freeze response. This alarm system becomes perfected and activates when anything feels familiar in the environment, thereby continuing to feed the soul (the mind, emotions, and intellect) and the somatic responses in the body.

Internal messages of fear cloud a person's ability to stand in biblical truth and to hear the voice of the Holy Spirit. This is part of Satan's plan to drown out the truth with lies that eventually imprison a person in shame.

THE CHURCH'S MISGUIDED RESPONSE

Let us now consider the church's response to this process. People share with me through their tears, "I'm supposed to pray it all away, and I am trying." The question that follows is: "What is wrong with me if I'm doing what I'm told to do, but it's not working?" The church compounds the internal messaging of "I am defective" with methods that bring condemnation.

This is the opposite of God's mercy, which meets individuals exactly where they are to bring healing to their souls and bodies. God wants to bring truth to people's souls, and the body of Christ is meant to carry comfort to the soul and spirit and lead people to the work of the cross through approaches rooted in both love and truth.

I have seen that when we help with the healing of past wounds held in a person's body and soul, ears that could not hear and eyes that could not see begin to experience an awakening to the leading of the Holy Spirit, the greatest Counsellor (John 14:16–17, 26; 15:26; 16:7 CSB). I have witnessed the interwoven experience of suffering and healing in the spirit, soul, and body in session with clients. It has been my observation that suffering held in the mind and the body holds people in captivity. A holistic approach involving a relationship built on trust and vulnerability as well as integrative neuroscience treatment rooted in Scripture can bring healing.

The healing of the soul weaves into the healing of the body, and the healing of the body and the soul is woven into how people experience their spiritual life with the Lord. The healing of wounds in the mind and the body brings realignment to the proper order of our created design to know Christ and be led by the Spirit of the living God.

Chapter Three Notes

_____

_____

_____

_____

_____

_____

_____

_____

_____

_____

_____

_____

_____

_____

_____

_____

_____

_____

_____

_____

_____

CHAPTER FOUR

Led by the Spirit

My clients enter my office, seeking comfort and answers for some of life's most challenging questions. I can see the pain inscribed upon their faces. The prospect of gaining hope rises when someone is willing to listen and engage with their stories. This stage is precious because it reveals that when we feel that all is lost, we can still hold on to "faith, hope and love" (1 Corinthians 13:13).

GOD'S ROLE IN PAIN

When we lead from this posture of understanding as disciples of Christ in all our spheres of influence, it allows people to engage their deeper hurts and questions. It creates a space that invites people to bring questions about God's role in their pain.

I am asked many variations of the following daunting questions: Where is God? How could He allow such suffering? If God has allowed this pain to come into my life, does He still love me? Will He answer my prayers? If the Scriptures are true, then what is wrong with me?

I hear scriptures quoted alongside these questions, such as "And the peace of God, which transcends all understanding, will guard your hearts and your minds in Christ Jesus" (Philippians 4:7) and "'For I know the plans I have for you,' declares the LORD, 'plans to prosper you and not to harm you, plans to give you hope and a future'" (Jeremiah 29:11).

When people feel that these scriptures do not fit with their own experiences in life, they begin to think, "If God is good, then something must be really wrong with me." They may start to believe the lies that they were made to suffer, that they were designed to live with mental illness, or that they need to try harder to do good works because God does not love them.

LIVING IN LIMBO

God is not the author of pain, but ever since the fall of humanity (Genesis 3), pain has been a reality in our world. Sadly, this pain may cause people to believe that God has forsaken them, and then the lies created by Satan overtake them. They may leave the church or even give up on their relationship with God altogether. Many Christians live in a state of dissonance, with competing beliefs causing them to wander in the wilderness. It feels like they are living in limbo, and their faith is barely holding on, like the generation of Israelites who were delivered from Egypt but never saw the promised land.

The wilderness is full of fear, shame, condemnation, and the perspective that God is a distant God. Many Christians find themselves in this place at some point, but it is not a place that God intends or expects for them to stay. God does not mean for His children to wander in endless pain. There is a way out, but fear is debilitating.

THE STRATEGY OF FEAR

In earlier chapters, we explored how the root of suffering within our mental health is a brain wired by fear-based responses. Fear reflects an individual's experiences, and when the brain is reminded of those experiences, it creates a survival plan that is helpful to it. However, the survival strategies of the brain are not beneficial to the person's ability to function and live in a place of peace.

Satan's greatest plan to sabotage the body of Christ is to evoke fear that sends individual believers into a wilderness filled with dense fog that causes them to see, hear, and experience only their suffering. When people stay too long in this fog, they come to believe that God has forsaken them and that they are destined to live a burdened and hopeless life. Most importantly, Satan wants Christians to question God's character.

HOPELESSNESS AND DESPAIR

On July 22, 1996, I wrote a journal entry during a season when the fog was so dense that I stopped believing I was worth anything. This entry was marked by the past tense because I no longer believed that my hopes would come to fruition. My life was surrounded by fear as I was in an abusive relationship with a young man from my church youth group whom I had married at a young age.

My pain was so unbearable that I believed that all my dreams and hopes had died. I wrote, "I wanted to help people in ways that people could trust me. I wanted to show them that life is worth more than destroying it and others. Through each situation, I wanted to show them that every person could pass on their love and the things they learned about life to others. It would be a huge line of people learning and growing from the love and support of others."

When I wrote that journal entry, I had come to the point where I believed that my life would not amount to anything with purpose or worth. My dreams for my future became hopeless and empty. I journeyed in survival mode, feeling numb. When uncomfortable experiences and emotions surfaced, I would self-harm, taking everything out on myself.

GOD NEVER ABANDONS HIS CHILDREN

This sense of hopelessness gripped my life long after I left that abusive marriage. I then created a mindset that God did not understand me and had left me. I came to believe that "I was created only to determine how much one could suffer" (a quotation from my journal). These lies followed me for years.

One night, as I sat on my bedroom floor, I opened the Bible to Romans 7:14–25. It was the first time I had felt that God heard my inner struggles and did not come to chastise or condemn me. My Abba, my Father, placed His hands under my chin to raise my eyes so that I would look upon my Saviour. God revealed His character to me that night, and I experienced validation regarding the battle within my soul and body. He reminded me that this was why He had given me His Son, Jesus, as His redemptive plan out of His love for me.

THE FLESH VERSUS THE SPIRIT

Years of observing and listening to clients and reflecting on my own story brought me to the revelation of why the body of Christ does not live in "the peace of God, which transcends all understanding" (Philippians 4:7) and worship like the Apostle Paul did while in prison (Acts 16:16–40). The word of God describes being led by the Holy Spirit, and we are made as three-part beings of spirit, soul, and body (1 Thessalonians 5:23; Hebrews 4:12; 1 Samuel 1:15; Isaiah 26:9). However, as Galatians 5:17–18 tells us, "The flesh desires what is contrary to the Spirit, and the Spirit what is contrary to the flesh. They are in conflict with each other, so that you are not to do whatever you want. But if you are led by the Spirit, you are not under the law."

We have free will to make choices, and our souls and bodies always want to take control of our spirits. The battle is real within each of us. Our fallen souls oppose the work of the Holy Spirit.

LOVED TO BE LOVING

In Romans 7, Paul described the struggle that we all face. When the Lord led me to this passage of Scripture, it validated how difficult it was for me to live a life that honoured God. That moment was my first experience of God's steadfast love, truth, and faithfulness reaching down and providing me with the gift of mercy.

Psalm 85:10–11 tells us, "Steadfast love and truth and faithfulness meet together; righteousness and peace kiss each other. Truth springs from the earth, and righteousness looks down from heaven" (AMP). How beautiful is this scripture that reveals the Father's character and heart for His children! God loves us, and His love teaches us how to love other people. We are loved so that we can be loving toward others.

God wants us to walk in Christlike character, developing and demonstrating the fruit of the Spirit (Galatians 5:22–23). We cannot become like Christ without intimacy with our Saviour and community with other believers. This is the only path that leads us to experience peace beyond all understanding. If we understand that Jesus has won the battle within us and we can lean upon Him during our most difficult seasons, then we are able to rest in His love.

THE BATTLE RAGES ON

The Spirit-led life is not a passive journey but one that is flooded with conflict. The internal battle between the flesh (the soul and the body) and the spirit is ongoing, as Paul described. Believers in Jesus Christ are called to be led by the Spirit (Romans 8:14) and to die to self, taking up their crosses daily to follow Jesus (Luke 9:23–25). This requires an attitude of willing obedience to follow the leading of the Holy Spirit even when conflict and suffering ensue. When we choose to follow Jesus and "do not turn to the right or the left" (Proverbs 4:25–27), we will experience God's peace, which is beyond our understanding. During our darkest moments, our Saviour does not look away, but joins us in the storm (Mark 4:35–41; 6:45–52).

THE DARKEST STORM

On February 10, 2009, I experienced the darkest storm of my life. It was the day I sat in the doctor's office with the unimaginable fear of something being very wrong with my son. It was the day I heard, "We think your son has Acute Lymphoblastic Leukemia." Acute Lymphoblastic Leukemia (ALL) is a type of cancer of the blood and bone marrow. The bloodwork was done immediately. One hour later, when I was at home, the devastation of the doctor's words was confirmed as I stood in my kitchen on a personal phone call with the doctor.

I cried and screamed uncontrollably. I never imagined that this would be part of my life. I blamed God and became angry with Him. I lost my footing and remembrance of God's character.

Thus began what would become a three-year journey that was relentlessly draining as we travelled the depressing hospital halls three times a week for treatment. We endured numerous rushed emergency admittances in the middle of the night with our son and fifteen-month-old daughter, and I was pregnant during the first nine months of our son's treatment. My personal experiences are akin to the Mother's Day commercial for Sick Kids Toronto, which shows a mom crying in the shower but getting up to fight another day.[20]

FROM BAD TO WORSE

The battle for my son's life was intense. Three years into this journey, with only six months left of active treatment, we thought that we were almost done. My fight was being done in the flesh, and it was a heavy burden. At the three-year mark, I was at work and heard a knock on my door. I will never forget the look on my husband's face. He pulled me out into the hall and shared that our son's cancer had returned. During a routine assessment, it was discovered that our son had relapsed in his central nervous system.

We were faced with a panel of doctors asking us to choose between intensive chemo and radiation or bone marrow transplant and radiation. How do you go about choosing?

Our only question to the panel of doctors was: "What is the most curable option?" We decided on a bone-marrow transplant that led us to live at Sick Kids Toronto and Ronald McDonald House for four months with our son and two daughters. My husband and I were both self-employed and could not work as we needed to focus on our children. We were able to access some funds through an amazing sponsorship family and fundraising efforts, yet we came close to losing our home.

FIGHTING OR TRUSTING

I battled with questions, suffering, and bitterness. I lived in a wilderness season filled with fear and anger. I willingly lived outside of the leading of the Spirit due to false and distorted beliefs I held regarding God's character. My husband and I had a routine of alternating one night at the hospital with our son and the following night at Ronald McDonald House with our daughters. We felt like two ships passing in the night as we switched off to ensure that our children always had one of their parents.

One evening, while alone at Ronald McDonald House, I sat at the kitchen table after tucking my girls into bed. I placed my hands on my cheeks and closed my eyes, shedding tears of deep pain. I prayed the most earnest of prayers to my heavenly Father, my Abba, because I could no longer carry this burden alone. At that moment, Holy Spirit led me to surrender my son at the cross. I thought that my son would die, and I had to come to terms with that. As I write this sentence,

I recall the very moment when I took my son and passed him over to God as though I was Abraham laying down his son Isaac. I said, "Your will be done." No matter what the ending would be, I had to trust God.

I could not fight anymore, and I chose to trust God. I will never forget the peace that flooded me on the inside when I chose to align my will with the leading of the Holy Spirit. That night, I decided to trust in God's character even if I could not understand His ways or plans. Peace arose within me and caused the darkness of fear to leave. God's perfect love drove out my fear (1 John 4:18) so that I could run with perseverance and courage.

The Lord gave me the strength to continue with confidence in Him. The journey was still difficult, but I knew that my Father was with me and was storing all my tears in a bottle (Psalm 56:8 NLT). I have been gifted and designed with the same emotions as you. I felt them deeply and often. But there was a resounding difference of inner peace when I aligned my will and thoughts to God's character. It felt like Jesus was carrying me even though the storm was raging around me. I still had sadness and pain, but there was also a sense that I was in the Lord's hands and I could trust Him.

I am happy to say that my son is doing well today, but I also know of families that have lost their children. My point here is that I had to trust that if the Lord took my son, I could still know that God loves my son and me and would carry me through my grieving and trials.

LED BY THE SPIRIT

If we are to be led by the Spirit, we must trust the Spirit. Our circumstances will not always be what we want them to be, but faith means that we trust God no matter what. Matthew 4:1 tells us that "Jesus was led by the Spirit into the wilderness to be tempted by the devil." God did not cause the temptation, but He was sovereign over it (as with Job). Sometimes the Spirit will lead you into difficult trials. When Jesus was led by the Spirit in Matthew 4, it was not sunshine and rainbows; it was fasting, hunger, and trials. God's leading can take us to seasons of testing and refining (Malachi 3:2–3; Zechariah 13:9).

Trusting God does not make us immune to pain or suffering. However, God did give me internal peace in the midst of suffering. Like the woman in the song by Carrie Underwood, I came to a place where I had to say, "Jesus take the wheel."[21] I wanted to be in control, but instead I let go and trusted God to guide me.

LOGIC VERSUS LEANING

God is calling us to "walk by faith, not by sight" (2 Corinthians 5:7 NKJV), which means that we cannot rely on our own logic (in the prefrontal cortex area of the brain). Instead, we need to trust in God's character and the leading of the Holy Spirit: "Trust in the LORD with all your heart and lean not on your own understanding; in all your ways submit to him, and he will make your paths straight" (Proverbs 3:5–6).

When we choose every day to "fight the good fight of the faith" (1 Timothy 6:12), even when conflict and suffering occur, we are choosing to be led by the Spirit and to live in a place of hope. Romans 5:5 assures us that "hope does not put us to shame, because God's love has been poured out into our hearts through the Holy Spirit, who has been given to us."

Many people in our churches are weighed down by their suffering. They need to experience God's love being poured into their hearts through the Holy Spirit, and this may begin in a relationship with a willing vessel inside the walls of the church. When we serve as vessels of God's love for other people and lead them by the hand toward our Saviour, we are bringing love and truth together.

THE CHURCH IS A HOSPITAL

The church is a hospital for the broken-hearted that helps to lead people to Jesus, the perfect salve for the soul. Relationship is the primary vehicle that opens the door to receiving love and grace. The revelation that "perfect love drives out fear" (1 John 4:18) is difficult to comprehend in an environment that is not authentic and vulnerable. Every leader and congregant will experience seasons that challenge one or multiple parts of his or her tripartite being (spirit, soul, and body). Job lamented in his time of great suffering, "Therefore I will not restrain my mouth [body]; I will speak in the anguish of my spirit; I will complain in the bitterness of my soul" (Job 7:11 NKJV).

It is not helpful to tell a person who has been diagnosed with cancer to focus only on the leading of the Spirit through more prayer and more faith. We expect people to access medical treatment from doctors if their bodies are sick, but that does not mean that they do not have faith to believe. Similarly, people battling mental illness should not be told to neglect decades of insights from health professionals because all they need is more faith.

CONNECTION AND COMPASSION

A holistic approach for our churches starts with connection and compassion. We should strive to cultivate vulnerability in our churches so that healthy relationships can blossom. As Brené Brown writes in her book *Daring Greatly*, "Vulnerability is the birthplace of love, belonging, joy, courage, empathy, and creativity. It is the source of hope, empathy, accountability, and authenticity. If we want greater clarity in our purpose or deeper and more meaningful spiritual lives, vulnerability is the path."[22]

We need vulnerable and compassionate relationships that help people to engage the hard questions in ways that lead them to Jesus in truth and love rather than away from Him in shame and condemnation. Jesus said, "He who believes in Me [who adheres to, trusts in, and relies on Me], as the Scripture has said, 'From his innermost being will flow continually rivers of living water'" (John 7:38 AMP). This living water is the Holy Spirit that flows through us and, more importantly, is expressed through us to others. This expression reveals the heart of God. It means that He entrusts us as vessels for His kingdom.

A holistic plan for healing is shaped by a greater awareness of where each person needs to begin. For example, if someone is battling sickness in the body, you can pray with that person and accompany him or her to hospital appointments. Someone who is battling depression needs a voice of compassion and prayer and a plan to access treatment by a trained Christian therapist.

If we affirm the truth of the Bible, then we cannot deny that we are to be led by the Holy Spirit (Psalm 143:10; John 16:13–15; Romans 5:5; Romans 8:14; Galatians 5:16–18). However, following the Spirit's leading is possible only if we choose to keep our eyes on Jesus. The church is supposed to be "equipping ... the saints for the work of ministry" (Ephesians 4:12 NKJV), and we need to seek methods that draw people to intimacy with Jesus and the resulting process of sanctification instead of creating shame. In this way, the body of Christ "grows and builds itself up in love" (Ephesians 4:16).

Chapter Four Notes

CHAPTER FIVE

A Model of Care

Before we discuss a transformative model of care, we need to begin by reflecting on our own experiences. Who has been a helpful support in your life? Where do you go for counsel and encouragement?

When you sought counsel and shared what you were going through, what was the experience like for you? Did you feel known and seen, without someone else's expectations or preconceptions? Did you feel heard before insight or advice was given? Did you experience a compassionate, humble, gentle, loving, relational interaction?

If so, did this encourage you to continue to seek help and increase your desire to know the Lord? Alternatively, if you had a negative experience that brought you pain, what made you feel unheard and unseen, maybe even shamed or condemned?

We should reflect upon our own experiences of receiving help to give it correctly. What was truly helpful, and what was hurtful? The answers can help us to treat other people the way we want to be treated.

GO BACK TO GO FORWARD

Unresolved experiences from our past determine how we respond and lead in relationships with people who are hurting. In *Emotionally Healthy Spirituality*, Peter Scazzero writes that "the work of growing in Christ (what theologians [and the Bible] call sanctification) does not mean we don't go back to the past as we press ahead to what God has for us. It actually demands we go back in order to break free from unhealthy and destructive patterns that prevent us from loving ourselves and others as God designed."[23]

When we adopt this concept for ourselves, we can lead from a place of empathy and compassion as we seek to help people who are hurting. However, if we do not go back before attempting to go forward, we risk causing harm because our own wounds may blind us.

THE WAITING ROOM EXPERIENCE

Most people enter the counselling meeting with both trepidation and hope. When people invite another human being into the vulnerable parts of their lives, they fear risking their safety and identity. At my office, the waiting room serves as a symbolic place of safety that invites people to feel supported. We use calming colours and a relaxed living-room setting to convey these sentiments. This space reveals that our hearts are open to hear and receive.

However, we are deeply aware that this environment alone cannot penetrate the thick walls of self-protection or shame that have been built up over the years. When we, as therapists, enter the waiting room, we can see expressions of pain displayed on people's faces. We can see that they are scared to open this figurative door of trust. How we approach new clients for the first time can impact whether they open up or stay closed.

The common ground for all people entering counselling is that they are experiencing the results of wounds. These wounds of rejection, betrayal, and abandonment can be actual or perceived. In the waiting room, people grapple with the feelings of whether their relationship with their helper (therapist, pastor, or another leader) will feel safe and supportive.

They begin assessing this relationship from the moment of entry because the human brain categorizes and evaluates any similarities perceived as markers of past experiences. The brain and nervous system have rehearsed and perfected this systematic assessment. Through the helper's non-verbal and verbal communication cues, the entrance sets the stage for whether this person will choose vulnerability. Even the foyer can communicate, "I am for you. I am here to help you. You are safe here."

The First Point of Contact

As a result, the first point of contact should be handled carefully. This is the moment when people reach out for help. It could be an email, a phone call, or entering into our physical space at the church or office. This is our first opportunity to reflect the hands of grace in both disposition and character and to reveal an open stance that offers safety. We need to enter this sacred space of connection through a loving approach. Then we can engage in the process of building a trusting relationship that allows for the opportunity to teach, challenge, pray, and move toward healing.

James 3:17 states, "But the wisdom from above is first of all pure. It is also peace loving, gentle at all times, and willing to yield to others. It is full of mercy and the fruit of good deeds. It shows no favoritism and is always sincere" (NLT). We must lead from a place of gentleness, with the willingness to yield to clients. Without this firm foundation of a relationship, we will not be given the opportunity to help.

Proverbs 11:14 reveals that "where there is no [wise, intelligent] guidance, the people fall [and go off course like a ship without a helm], but in the abundance of [wise and godly] counselors there is victory" (AMP). When wounded people enter a helping process, they do so with deep-seated fear in their souls and bodies, and Satan tries to use that fear to destroy their lives.

In 2011, when I felt God leading me to begin building a therapeutic practice, I had a deep desire to reveal the heart and love of Jesus. I wanted to communicate this through our website, engaging spaces, and sensitivity to building trust and relationships with hurting people. While developing my website, I came across an anonymous quotation that resonated with my desire to help: "A willingness to listen, a pair of helping hands, a whisper from the heart from someone who cares and understands." This is posted on our home page.

Being invited into the deepest parts of another person's life should never be minimized or taken for granted. This is the moment when a person is willing to engage in a difficult and complex process.

JOIN PEOPLE IN THEIR MUD

I often use a simple analogy with my clients to describe the themes I have seen throughout my decades of work. I tell everyone that we all have experiences that have been painful, traumatic, and negative. When not healed, these painful experiences are like mud that accumulates through the years. The mud feels painful, heavy, and burdensome. We feel it and see it, but we want to ignore it.

Most of us would prefer to jump over or run around this mud by focusing on areas of our lives that feel less daunting. To suppress the pain, we spend more time perfecting our cooking or public-speaking skills. We stay busy, or we use distractions or substances. However, each time we suppress, ignore, fight, or flee, we are brought back to our unresolved past experiences through reminders, triggers, and a history of pain that has not yet been resolved.

The mud symbolizes our past experience of adverse events

and trauma and the choices we make to soothe the wounds caused by others. In countless homes and offices, we can see people's efforts to bury themselves under paperwork, yard work, and housework as a means of avoidance. Viewing highlight reels on social media reinforces the belief that we are not good enough and need to hide. Binge-watching of TV shows, addictions, and procrastination can all be forms of denial and evasion.

The ache is held in the form of humour, divisive conversations, extroversion, and introversion, and it does not move. A maladaptive cycle of more activity or less activity never brings an antidote to the pain but only causes the merry-go-round to continue without slowing. These emotions, physical sensations, and beliefs cannot be healed through logic and reason. Our pain must be experienced and held by another caring person. It is easier to remain stuck in a cycle of avoidance when we choose to walk alone or if our helpers do not understand that the way we appear on the surface may be a cover for deep hurt. We need people to sit with us to face our pain.

A compassionate and loving model of care always begins with a focus on how and where we start together. We need to stop looking at how we experience healing and resolution at the end and instead learn to engage people at the beginning of the process without assumptions.

We need to engage hurting people just as Jesus did with the Samaritan woman at the well (John 4:1–42). We must lean toward broken-hearted individuals with the willingness to walk with them while displaying Christlike character. Are we clothed "with compassion, kindness, humility, gentleness and patience" (Colossians 3:12)? Do we desire to listen lovingly to other people so they can process their pain?

Our job is to get past the walls that people create so we can help from the inside out. We do not stand on the outside, looking in, with a pointed finger, shaming words, and condemning remarks. We enter this sacred space of vulnerability and stay with people in their mud until they walk out of it in the revelatory power of the Holy Spirit, the greatest Counsellor and Teacher (John 14:16–17, 26 CSB).

BUILD LOVING RELATIONSHIPS

We all have to enter the mud of our past so we can one day walk out of the mud permanently. We are not asking individuals to do this work alone; we are choosing to partner with them in their pain. Christians are the hands and feet of Jesus in this world, and this ministry is relational (1 Corinthians 12:27; John 13:35). Beyond feeding the hungry, we are called to build relationships with those in need (Luke 14:12–14; James 1:27).

We are often wounded within the context of relationships. Therefore, building non-judgemental, safe, compassionate relationships is essential to leading people to the cross, where they can surrender their lives completely. When we demonstrate the fruit of the Spirit (Galatians 5:22–23), we are revealing the image of the One who came to save us from our burdens. Jesus said, "Come to me, all you who are weary and burdened, and I will give you rest. Take my yoke upon you and learn from me, for I am gentle and humble in heart, and you will find rest for your souls" (Matthew 11:28–29). We are following Christ when we walk humbly with those who are hurting to help carry their burdens (Galatians 6:2).

When we approach people with grace and mercy, we foster calmness and openness and encourage people to engage with stories full of the perceptions and truth they hold in their souls (the mind, will, and emotions) and bodies (the brain and nervous system). This begins the process of healing. Many people have never shared their stories, because shame silences them. We open the door to healing when we sincerely desire to know people and are willing to show up without judgemental language.

A PLACE OF UNDERSTANDING

The challenge for every helper (therapist, pastor, or leader) is understanding how the interwoven nature of the spirit, soul, and body hinders or helps people to heal. Using a one-dimensional framework for the helping process leads people to believe that they are suffering in only one part of their tripartite being. We must address the whole person in order to facilitate the healing process.

Throughout my years as a practicing registered social worker and psychotherapist, many Christians have sat on my couch and described the countless methods they have tried to find healing and transformation. Clients have taken part in deliverance sessions, inner-healing conferences, prayer, and

Bible reading. The reoccurring theme was that they believed they would never escape their struggles, because these previous experiences had limited results and their suffering continued. Satan's lies built up over time and took them down the path of hopelessness.

Various methods can be helpful, but the church has ignored the research surrounding how the brain and nervous system hold negative and traumatic events. This is why we must not only address spiritual matters with prayer and studying the Bible, but also give attention to the mind and body. That way, we can meet people where they are in their journey and offer true help from a place of understanding.

EYE MOVEMENT DESENSITIZATION AND REPROCESSING (EMDR)

One of the most profound experiences I have witnessed was when a woman was processing a traumatic memory of abuse through a type of therapy called Eye Movement Desensitization and Reprocessing (EMDR). This method helps to rewire the brain and discharge the nervous system, allowing the person to heal through experiencing the unresolved trauma and then letting it go.[24]

The most intense experience that moved us emotionally occurred when the Holy Spirit brought truth through a scripture she had memorized years ago as a child. Her ears could hear the truth found in the "still small voice" (1 Kings 19:12 NKJV) only after her brain and nervous system had removed the symptoms of trauma through EMDR.

She excitedly shared that she had forgotten that scripture, but it had profound meaning for her when she was restored from the pain of abuse. When she realized that Jesus loved her deeply, she shed tears of joy. Before that moment, her bodily pain and internalized trauma had prevented her from standing on this truth. Once she experienced healing in her soul and body, her spirit could take the lead.

She shared during her therapy that she was often shamed by others and believed that she was a bad Christian because so many leaders in the church could not figure out why she did not get better. This kind of direct or indirect messaging causes people to believe that the church is not a place to seek help, often leading people to flounder or seek help in the wrong places. They are shamed into believing that they are not doing enough or that they are bad people. This mindset does not reflect the saving grace and mercy of Jesus.

MY OWN TRAUMA

When I went through several traumatic experiences over the course of my son's sickness, I knew that I was suffering from PTSD. My son was only three years old, and his veins were collapsing because the doctors drew so much blood. I was a wreck emotionally and was drained after so many months of various procedures for him, including chemotherapy. I was also devastated by the haunting feelings of helplessness. I would do anything to help my son, even give my own life, but I knew that I could not heal him.

To make matters worse, when the doctors wheeled my son into surgery, he was not yet sedated and continually screamed for me. It was excruciatingly painful to hear his tearful cries of "Mommy! Mommy!" but I could not do anything to alleviate his fear and pain. I could not go with him or answer his cry for help but only stand there and watch him disappear behind the large double doors of the surgery room.

On that occasion, I felt so desperate that I stopped the doctors from taking my son into surgery. I then ran into the bathroom with my husband's sweater, took my shirt off, put on the sweater, and ran back to give my son my shirt. I thought that it might provide a little comfort to a toddler who did not fully grasp what was happening. At least he could have a part of me with him. As traumatic as this was for him, I was traumatized, too. There were also the unknowns of what would happen to my son and whether this storm would ever end.

I was a trained and certified EMDR therapist at that time and knew the profound effects this method could have in processing trauma. Through that experience, I was able to deal with many traumatic symptoms. I no longer felt shame and could walk in freedom. This process addressed my spirit, soul, and body and helped me to experience God's mercy and grace. God met me exactly where I was and told me to pass all the unknowns and pain over to Him. The burden lifted, and I felt an incredible peace.

I believe that some of this healing took place because the therapist was relational. She did not act like a professional who had all the answers. Instead, she built an organic relationship with me. She asked me how I was doing and actually wanted an honest answer. She demonstrated God's love by getting to know me and how I felt. She took the necessary time to do so, never rushing, and was always focused on the session.

She also showed me that God was always with my son, even when I could not be. God was holding my son and me at the same time, and this helped me to let go of the feeling of helplessness. I no longer felt like my son was alone in a hospital room, because I trusted that our heavenly Father was with him.

The trauma had led me to believe that God had forsaken me, but the therapist showed me that God was with me, just as He was with Jesus when He felt forsaken. Like in the "Footprints (in the Sand)" poem, I sensed that God had not left me during this painful season but was holding me. However, I could not feel or believe this until I went through the EMDR process and the trauma was released from my body.

All of this led me to wonder how many Christians were being told only to read the Bible and pray more when something else might be beneficial. Prayer and God's word can have healing effects, to be sure, but pushing people in a direction that is not working reveals a lack of awareness that undermines relationship and healing.

A NEW APPROACH

If Christians simply quote the Bible, it can come across as legalistic and impersonal. We need to lead with a relational focus. We should use the Bible while counselling but must also keep many other issues in mind. For instance, are we being attentive and compassionate? Are we fully present, or do we seem rushed or distracted? Are we showing that we sincerely care about the person? Are we giving validation and helping the person to know his or her value? Are we treating the person as an individual who may not fit certain stereotypes? Does the person feel connected to us, or are we trying to rush him or her out of the office?

When we treat people like items to check off a list and try to complete the task of helping them with a quick wave of a Bible verse, we come across as uncaring. That type of help is not truly helpful and can actually cause harm. Are we taking the time to listen to people's stories and empathize, or do we want to solve problems quickly? Without building trust and encouraging people to open up, we cannot get to the root of the problem to be solved.

Are we meeting people where they are or pushing people to where we want them to be? Are we using the Bible in a judgemental way or in a loving and restorative way? We can hurt people by using our sermons or counselling to cover up our own hurts. We may do unhealthy things if we are blind to our own mud and aspects of our stories, unknowingly allowing them to spill into our work and ministry. We may be funnelling our wounds into our sermons or advice if we have unresolved pain. We can come across as self-righteous or prideful because we have not gone through a healing process ourselves.

The church needs to recognize that seeking support

through counsel does not mean that the living word of God is not enough or that the Holy Spirit cannot lead people to change. Counselling is about meeting people where they are rather than where we think they should be. We do not believe in a one-size-fits-all solution and instead take the time to assess what each person needs most, addressing the soul and the body as well as the spirit.

MALLEABLE VESSELS OF GOD

The Apostle Paul chose to "become all things to all people" so that he might win more for the kingdom of God (1 Corinthians 9:22). He wrote:

> *Even though I am free of the demands and expectations of everyone, I have voluntarily become a servant to any and all in order to reach a wide range of people: religious, non-religious, meticulous moralists, loose-living immoralists, the defeated, the demoralized—whoever. I didn't take on their way of life. I kept my bearings in Christ—but I entered their world and tried to experience things from their point of view. I've become just about every sort of servant there is in my attempts to lead those I meet into a God-saved life. I did all this because of the Message. I didn't just want to talk about it; I wanted to be in on it!*
> *—1 Corinthians 9:19–23 (MSG)*

Paul wanted to reach more people with the gospel of Christ by meeting them exactly as and where they were. The church needs to realign itself to build bridges into the lives of the wounded. God is the author of salvation, and He uses followers of Christ to draw people to Him. We need to position ourselves as vessels of His love.

A Long-Term Mindset

Proverbs 11:30 teaches us that "the fruit of the [consistently] righteous is a tree of life, and he who is wise captures and wins souls [for God—he gathers them for eternity]" (AMP). How do we create an environment in which we can accomplish this purpose? Clients have sat on my couch and shared countless stories of judgement expressed by their church leadership and the shame they felt as a result. The church is filled with messages of sin and repentance and the supposed ease of simply "getting clean" or "getting better," as if transformation is supposed to happen overnight for everyone.

My experience in mental health is that healing is not an overnight process, but one that takes a caring person in a long-term partnership with the hurting person. We enter into this relationship when we care for the soul and the body of another person, not the spirit alone.

I have seen new helpers enter into this relationship with a to-do list based on preconceived ideas of how to solve what they assume to be the problem. I often say, "We need to get ourselves out of the way." When we learn to set our assumptions aside and slow down the process, we can be present in the here and now, occupying the same space as the other person and listening more than prescribing. This approach establishes the relationship necessary for truly helping some-one toward healing.

USING THE RIGHT SKILL SET CAREFULLY

One of the skills taught to me in university was knowing how to challenge our clients. It is an essential skill set as there are times throughout the process when this is desirable, de-pending on what surfaces in the healing journey. However, use of this skill set must coincide with a therapeutic relation-ship built on vulnerability, safety, and trust. We are able to speak "the truth in love" (Ephesians 4:15) to those who are in need within the parameters of this relationship.

In his book *The Meaning of Marriage*, Timothy Keller wrote, "Love without truth is sentimentality; it supports and affirms us but keeps us in denial about our flaws. Truth with-out love is harshness; it gives us information but in such a way that we cannot really hear it."[25] This is a universal principle for all relationships. Understanding how to communicate the truth from a place of love in the context of helping relation-ships is vital to staying in the mud with people without causing them to feel condemnation and shame that triggers a flight-or-fight response. Below are two lists to keep in mind when seeking to counsel people.

Shaming

1. Holding a belief that people should be healed after only a few support sessions.

2. Challenging a person immediately through direct words and advice instead of first building a trusting relationship.

3. Believing that Bible verses and prayer are the only path to healing.

4. Employing helping approaches that do not align with how trauma is stored in the body (the brain and nervous system). You cannot always talk it out of someone.

5. Displaying harshness in non-verbal and verbal behaviours.

Helpful

1. Building a trusting relationship at the beginning based on attunement, validation, and listening. It takes a few meetings to establish the relationship of trust before the helper can begin challenging the person being helped.

2. Referring the person to a Christian therapist when issues are beyond your scope of practice.

3. Clothing yourself with compassion, patience, gentleness, humility, and love (Colossians 3:12).

4. Using a comprehensive and holistic approach to helping that includes the spirit, the soul, and the body in the care and treatment of a person.

5. Rebuke (challenge) with gentleness and at the appropriate time (Proverbs 15:1, 25:11; Galatians 6:1; 2 Timothy 2:24–25).

TRUTH AND LOVE

The truth is what sets people free (John 8:32), but people are blocked from receiving the truth if their bodies and minds are trapped in a cycle of fear-based responses. "Perfect love drives out fear" (1 John 4:18), but love is too often missing from Christians' attitudes toward the people who need it most.

The challenge to Christians is to engage broken people who are stuck in their mud by meeting them where they are and genuinely seeking to know them. We can never truly help someone if we do not understand that person, and we cannot understand someone if we bring judgement and assumptions instead of compassion and openness. When we respond in love and humility, with Christlike character, love will drive out fear. Then truth will expel doubts and deceptions from the devil, who will flee in the name of Jesus. It is only when we approach people in love that they can be set free with the truth.

Chapter Five Notes

PART C:
Limitations—How Religion Limits and Imprisons People

CHAPTER SIX

The Unbalanced Church

In these times of crisis, we should be like a light shining on a hill (Matthew 5:14), reflecting the gospel of Jesus Christ. However, increasing numbers of Christians are trapped in darkness due to mental health concerns. In order to fulfill Jesus' commission, we need to gain a deeper understanding of healing.

Jesus called us to serve in the harvest field (Matthew 9:38) and to "make disciples of all nations" (Matthew 28:19–20). This mission should not only encompass the traditional concepts related to discipleship, such as evangelism, baptism, teaching, and mentoring, but expand to addresses the whole person, including mental health.

HELPING THE HOPELESS

How can Christians set the captives free if they feel burdened and hopeless due to mental illness? Many believers

87

attend church services week after week, hoping that someone will notice their pain while they remain silent about their suffering. They return home to hollow rooms filled with broken dreams and fading visions of their future.

They wonder if God sees them, and they begin to question whether they really matter to anyone, even to God. They cling tightly to Jesus in the hope that one day He will set them free from this pain. However, as the belief that they are undeserving, insignificant, and worthless takes hold, they slowly forget what Jesus did for them on the cross.

The days feel like the movie *Groundhog Day*, and the relentless pain leads to isolation and silence. Life feels hopeless. For some, suicide seems to be the only way to escape the pain. We do not see or hear about pastors, leaders, and individuals in congregations slowly fading away. We are surprised when we discover that someone has been hospitalized or diagnosed or has committed suicide.

The church has missed the signs. We have lost touch with the language of vulnerability and instead created walls of shame. We have forgotten the importance of nurturing relationships rooted in unity and love. We have not built a house of safety where people feel accepted when they are suffering from mental illness.

BE AWARE OF TRIGGERS

All of us, at some point, have judged someone in the church without fully knowing his or her story. This tends to be someone who triggers our buttons of discomfort, leading us to incorrect perceptions. These perceptions are not founded on fact or communicating with the person who causes the triggers and distress.

This trigger could be a tone of voice, facial expression, disposition, or sex, and the list go on. Many facets of human behaviours and attributes can serve as triggers and lead to judgement. There were many times in my life when a male who acted with authority, using a loud tone and direct language, caused me to feel scared and reactionary.

I would feel fear and then judge this person without getting to know his story. It was only when I resolved my past experience of an abusive marriage that I could hear that person's story. I realized that my reactions and judgements were born from a protective place that shielded me. These reactions would not always be present, but when they arose, I realized that I needed to heal my wounds. This reminder helps me to recognize the stories hidden behind what people project to the world.

As a result of these projected behaviours, we keep people at arm's length, allowing us to peek safely from behind our walls to assess who and what is safe. How often are people at church protecting themselves by hiding behind their walls? Do we show the real us, or does our church culture help to maintain the figurative walls people hide behind?

LOOK BENEATH THE SURFACE

A church that does not build relationships encourages an environment in which people judge the surface view of one another, which produces an unbalanced approach to help-ing. Perceptions and judgements cause harm when we assume that we know other people based on their behaviours and external attributes, because people rarely show their vul-nerabilities in full view of the church.

On the other hand, when church leadership establishes and promotes an environment of safety and acceptance, this mindset flows to the rest of the congregation. People will begin to stay longer outside of their figurative walls to reveal painful stories that need to be lovingly heard and addressed by the body of Christ.

INCONGRUENT PERCEPTIONS

Christian suicide rates and the number of Christians with mental illnesses have increased dramatically in recent years. Several Lifeway Research studies have revealed inconsisten-cies between the perceptions of leadership and those of churchgoers.[26]

The studies indicated that 92% of pastors say that their church is equipped to care for a family that experiences the suicide of a loved one. However, only 4% of churchgoers who lost a loved one to suicide say that church leaders were aware of their loved one's struggles.

Furthermore, 46% of pastors versus 12% of churchgoers say that their church regularly addresses mental illness. "De-spite their best intentions, churches don't always know how to help those facing mental health struggles," said Scott McConnell, executive director of Lifeway Research.[27]

Churches tend to lean into an unbalanced approach to helping, which often leaves people feeling overwhelmed and unsupported. A survey of leaders found that 35% believed mental illness could be overcome with Bible study and prayer alone. Prayer and Bible study should be encouraged as our primary conduit to connecting with God. But if a loving and safe human relationship does not accompany this encouragement, the message of "do more spiritual stuff" can feel condemning and shaming.

IS YOUR CHURCH A SAFE PLACE?

Throughout the years that I have been practicing in mental health, I have seen more Christians accessing care outside of their church than from their church because the leaders, structures, and practices led them into further suffering. The explanations revealed on my couch are filled with messages of "I am not a good enough Christian," "I am embarrassed to share my story, because people are judgemental about mental illness," and "I question whether I should attend this particular church or any church at all."

I often share with people that condemnation and shame are partners that only cause a person to feel imprisoned. People resort to silence in their church when the symptoms of mental illness become overwhelming. A church should feel safe, as if it is a family gathering around you, full of people who are encouraging, praying, and fighting alongside you, but that is often not the case.

Mental illness has now been recognized as a feature of

religions that use a legalistic approach, unhealthy power structures, and fear-based teachings about hell and impurity. Jesus did talk about hell and purity, such as in Matthew 5, but how He spoke about them was different from how some pastors and church leaders speak about them.

Jesus did not use fear tactics and was not condemning when He spoke about difficult topics. He reserved His harshest rebukes and condemnation for hypocritical religious leaders who knew better and were leading people astray (Matthew 23). They were trying to justify people through the law, but the law can only condemn, not save (Romans 10:3–4; Galatians 2:16; Colossians 2:16–17). Only Jesus can save.

How Jesus interacted with the hurting and broken is quite different. He spoke with love and concern when confronting people living in sin, such as the women at the well (John 4:1–42). At the same time, He did challenge her with the truth. His love was not separated from the truth, nor vice versa. Balancing truth and love in what we say and how we say it is paramount. Grace does not water down truth, and truth does not negate grace.

Matthew tells us that a prophecy from Isaiah 42 was fulfilled in Christ because of how humbly and gently He dealt with people: "He will not crush the weakest reed or put out a flickering candle. Finally he will cause justice to be victorious. And his name will be the hope of all the world" (Matthew 12:20–21 NLT). Jesus invited the "weary and burdened" to find rest in Him (Matthew 11:28). He described Himself and His invitation to salvation in this way: "Take my yoke upon you and learn from me, for I am gentle and humble in heart, and you will find rest for your souls. For my yoke is easy and my burden is light" (Matthew 11:29–30).

RELIGIOUS TRAUMA

Researchers have discovered that post-traumatic stress disorder (PTSD) and complex post-traumatic stress disorder (CPTSD) can result from religious systems based on power and control tactics rooted in fear. In light of these symptoms, Dr. Marlene Winell developed the diagnosis of religious trauma syndrome (RTS).[28]

Dr. Winell demonstrated that a combination of toxic theology and authoritarianism inhibits the early development of healthy independent thinking and creates feelings of condemnation.[29] As you may recall from earlier chapters, our brains develop responses to protect us from perceived or real threats. Trauma was misunderstood until research was undertaken to improve understanding of its effects on the brain and nervous system.

This research has given us insight into the implications of religious systems that evoke fear and trauma:

> Religious trauma results from an event, series of events, relationships, or circumstances within or connected to religious beliefs, practices, or structures that is experienced by an individual as overwhelming or disruptive and has lasting adverse effects on a person's physical, mental, social, emotional, or spiritual well-being.[30]

The Global Center for Religious Research has explained that while the term *religious trauma syndrome* is commonly used, many clinicians and researchers are removing the word *syndrome*, which is "an outdated label that can actually be more detrimental than helpful."[31] The reason for this change is that religious trauma does not consistently present the same symptoms in every individual, as would be required for the diagnosis of a syndrome.

I will emphasize here that I do not align with all of the beliefs and ideological assumptions of non-Christian researchers or clinical settings that do not centre on Jesus. However, I do appreciate the need for their research, including research into the harmful effects of legalistic or authoritarian religious settings. I would suggest that the body of Christ take note, because if people are being harmed, something on our end needs to change.

Trauma in the Body

In his book *Waking the Tiger*, Peter Levine shows that trauma need not be obviously traumatic to be traumatizing. Trauma is determined by how the body responds to an incident, not the actual incident itself.[32] Our bodies, including the brain and nervous system, are designed to express and feel physical and emotional pain. However, people who have experienced trauma in a fear-filled environment may not be able to feel somatic information, because they have disassociated from their bodies. They may use cognitions to explain instead of feel. However, we must feel if we are to heal.

When I listen to hurting voices expressing their stories on my couch, they do not sound like the voices of people redeemed by the cross, but rather people who believe that their pain is greater than the pain that Jesus bore on the cross for all humanity. It is difficult to believe that God's love has accomplished so much at the cross when wounds are deep, scars of the past are unbearable, and the emotions of today determine the truth.

Abiding in the Vine

If Christians do not abide in the vine, where we experience the pruning process and grow in the fruit of the Spirit, we cannot help others to process their pain (John 15:1–17). We are called to Christlike character that can be produced only in a person who is being sanctified. However, this process must happen in the context of loving relationships. Trying to motivate sanctification through fear tactics will fail. I believe that we need to stop pointing fingers at others and instead begin by examining ourselves. Only then can we determine whether or not we are truly experiencing the journey of becoming Christlike (James 1:19–27).

Perfectionism Always Fails

Religious legalistic systems demand an unattainable level of perfection that distorts or negates the grace of Jesus Christ. Questioning, struggling with sin, and not maintaining assumed gender roles result in condemnation and shame. These teachings are rooted in the law and not in the words of Jesus Christ.

In Jamie Lee Finch's book *You Are Your Own*, she describes her upbringing as one that "concentrated in maintaining a morality measured by upholding societal decorum and traditional gender roles."[33] She needed grace to face her struggles but did not find it in the church.

Religious Trauma and Leaving the Faith

If you were to search the internet for books about religious abuse and trauma, it might shock you to find that the common theme is how to walk away from your Christian faith. The countless number of books advising readers that there is freedom and escape when they leave their Christian faith burdens my heart with sadness.

If we read these books, we can hear the voices of those who have experienced pain within the confines of the church, and we can learn how to respond to people's struggles in a way that leads to healing instead of further harm. After reading some of these books, I have been left wondering why the church has removed Jesus as the face of Christianity when He is the centre of it. He is the anchor that secures us in a chaotic world. So why do religious structures from the days of the Pharisees, the very ones Jesus criticized so strongly, continue to be present in the church today?

Balancing Grace and Truth

People are imprisoned by legalistic messages from the
church even though Jesus came to set people free through the
cross. Jesus took our sins, burdens, and despair to the cross,
but legalistic religious structures shackle people in hopelessness, in suffering, and sometimes in mental illness.

My challenge to every reader is to reclaim the Jesus of the
Bible, who came to walk with sinners and confront the Pharisees (Matthew 16:1–4; Matthew 22; Mark 10:2–9; Mark
12). In John 8, we read about Jesus' interaction with a woman
who was caught in adultery:

> *At dawn he appeared again in the temple courts, where all
> the people gathered around him, and he sat down to teach
> them. The teachers of the law and the Pharisees brought
> in a woman caught in adultery. They made her stand be-
> fore the group and said to Jesus, "Teacher, this woman was
> caught in the act of adultery. In the Law Moses com-
> manded us to stone such women. Now what do you say?"
> They were using this question as a trap, in order to have a
> basis for accusing him.*
>
> *But Jesus bent down and started to write on the ground
> with his finger. When they kept on questioning him, he
> straightened up and said to them, "Let any one of you who
> is without sin be the first to throw a stone at her." Again he
> stooped down and wrote on the ground.*
>
> *At this, those who heard began to go away one at a time,
> the older ones first, until only Jesus was left, with the
> woman still standing there. Jesus straightened up and
> asked her, "Woman, where are they? Has no one con-
> demned you?"*
>
> *"No one, sir," she said.*

"Then neither do I condemn you," Jesus declared. "Go now and leave your life of sin."

—John 8:2-11

We see our Saviour speak the truth with love, not using shaming or condemning words. In contrast, churches have often created structures that cast the first stone rather than speaking words of love, grace, and mercy that lead to truth. Remember that the truth will set people free only when we approach them in love. A religious, legalistic attitude leads to throwing the first stone, but if we follow Jesus, He will make us "fishers of men" (Matthew 4:19 NKJV).

PATTERNS OF PAIN

In 2011, God opened a door for me to hear stories of legalistic structures in the church. Client after client shared similar painful stories of control, abuse of power, shaming, condemnation, and fear tactics used by church leaders. Numbing stoicism had kept these individuals safe behind their walls. Every time I watched people cautiously share their stories, I saw the pain in their eyes.

After a long day, I felt a sadness deep within my spirt, soul, and body, and it became almost unbearable. I sought the will of the Lord in prayer about how to help people living in fear-bound, legalistic structures. What happened to the message of the grace and love of Jesus Christ?

Once I woke up at 5 a.m. on a cold Canadian morning. I sat in my living-room chair, feeling a profound heaviness. I was perplexed by the feeling and asked the Lord to reveal the source of this painful burden. The "still small voice" penetrated my spirit, and the Lord told me to go to my office to pray.

After dropping my children off at school, I went to my office and sat in my chair, ready to pray. While looking at my schedule, I was shown that my entire day was filled up with six clients bound in legalism and despair. This explained the heaviness I was feeling. The Lord directed me to pray for every client, and I sensed a change in my spirit. But I could not forget the unhealthy pattern that was so distinct. The church was sick.

THE LAW CANNOT SAVE

Religious control is rooted in fear, but the Bible tells us that "there is no fear in love" (1 John 4:18). If God is love (1 John 4:7–21), then why are His people living in or creating environments of fear?

We cannot be set free by the law, as it only tells us what to do and not to do. It is powerless to forgive us and set us free. The law is like a mirror. It shows us what we look like but cannot clean us up. This is why telling people who are hurting to pray more and read the Bible more is only heaping more law upon them.

The law was designed to point out our sins, but it was not intended to save and heal us (Romans 7:4–13; Galatians 2–3). This is why Paul wrote, "For sin shall no longer be your master, because you are not under the law, but under grace"

(Romans 6:14). Jesus took our sin and shame to the cross to forgive and redeem us because keeping the law could not, as human beings are incapable of achieving perfection. Jesus came to the earth to make our freedom possible and to tell us and show us how to be free.

Paul wrote that "now, by dying to what once bound us, we have been released from the law so that we serve in the new way of the Spirit, and not in the old way of the written code" (Romans 7:6). Through the indwelling of the Holy Spirit, believers have the authority and power to walk in complete wholeness, freedom, and peace beyond our understanding. As followers and imitators of Jesus Christ, let us be a church that casts out fear with love and walks in the Spirit.

A SOLUTION FOR THE CHURCH

The writings of the Apostle Paul have provided us with a solution for the problem of the legalistic church. He told us that we should "earnestly desire and strive for the greater gifts [if acquiring them is going to be your goal]. And yet I will show you a still more excellent way [one of the choicest graces and the highest of them all: unselfish love]" (1 Corinthians 12:31 AMP). All believers are an integral part of the body of Christ, and we should use our gifts to help each other in a way that brings glory to our Lord and Saviour (1 Corinthians 12). The most important building block of these relationships is love. We must build each other up through the love of God in order to strengthen the church as a whole.

First Corinthians 13 challenges the church to establish a

lasting foundation of love, cautioning us that without love, even the most impressive spiritual gifts are meaningless. This Scripture passage gives us a detailed description of love:

> *Love is patient and kind. Love is not jealous or boastful or proud or rude. It does not demand its own way. It is not irritable, and it keeps no record of being wronged. It does not rejoice about injustice but rejoices whenever the truth wins out. Love never gives up, never loses faith, is always hopeful, and endures through every circumstance. ... Three things will last forever—faith, hope, and love—and the greatest of these is love.*
> **—1 Corinthians 13:4–7, 13** (NLT)

If we want the heartbeat of the church to change, then we need to have the heartbeat of Jesus, who said, "By this everyone will know that you are my disciples, if you love one another" (John 13:35). A church that builds a foundation of love that mirrors Christ's love for the church will foster genuine, lasting healing and transformation, and this begins with church leadership.

THE WAY FORWARD

Below are some practical strategies to consider as we seek to rebuild our churches to reflect the heart of Christ.

1. We should never underestimate how our history determines the way we govern ourselves today. Every person should seek to understand how his or her past

influences behaviours and perspectives that then affect church doctrine and policies.

2. Leaders should access literature and research pertaining to religious trauma to ensure that the church is not leading in fear, but only in love.

3. Leaders in the church should openly communicate their support for Christian therapy and acknowledge that those who seek it do not have to feel ashamed about it. The church is a hospital for the brokenhearted, but even hospitals refer patients to specialists. Every leader and congregant should have the opportunity to seek wise counsel that leads to healing (Proverbs 11:14; 19:20).

4. Leadership should seek to create an environment of safety and vulnerability by sharing openly about their past and present suffering, shortcomings, and healing. Shame tells us to remain silent, but a redeemed past brings glory to God. We should all want to share our testimonies. Revelation 12:11 states, "And they overcame and conquered him because of the blood of the Lamb and because of the word of their testimony, for they did not love their life and renounce their faith even when faced with death" (AMP).

5. Leadership should seek to have an open dialogue about mental illness from a place of compassion. We must choose our words and tone carefully. We can challenge someone without talking about sin,

condemnation, or hell. This is not because we are watering down the truth, but because we want the person to listen without becoming defensive. Share that we want to help people in their struggles and lead them away from choices that will hurt them and their relationship with Jesus. Explain that we want to help people to honour Christ and grow closer to Him.

6. We must balance truth and love. Love without truth is sentimentalism and often leads to immorality, while truth without love is harsh and leads to condemnation.[34]

Change begins with awareness of the problem, and change in the prevalent mindsets within our churches is no different. Leaders need to ask themselves, "What kind of environment are we creating from the pulpit or in our offices?"

THE DREAM

Years ago, a client shared a profound dream that confirmed what our heavenly Father had been showing me. This client was raised in an extremely legalistic religious environment predominantly found in North America. In her dream, she was behind bars, without a key to escape. Jesus was outside the prison door, and He held the key to her freedom in His hand.

This dream confirmed all that I had witnessed and felt in my spirit. Out of our Father's love, He sent His only begotten

Son to save a lost world (John 3:16–17). The law could never do this (Romans 8:3). Only the sacrificial death and resurrection of Jesus Christ could. On the cross, Jesus redeemed a broken world. If we know that we have been redeemed by grace, why would we resort to the law to bring about the change that only God's grace can achieve?

This young woman has been set free ever since she experienced the Jesus of "yesterday and today and forever," who loves her deeply (Hebrews 13:8; Isaiah 61:1–3). Her freedom came as we partnered in relationship, session after session, for years, and she changed me, too. I experienced the power of a relationship in which one lays down one's life for another (John 15:12–13). I placed my perceptions, logic, and doctrine at the cross to seek first the Lord, who then demonstrated His love through me. The truth is that this client was my greatest teacher. She stretched me and helped me to reveal the fruit of the Spirit as I was led by Him in each session.

She needed to see Jesus, not religion, and I was willing to make myself invisible so I could serve as a reflection of Jesus' love. Through a relationship with me, this young woman saw Jesus. It was the love and truth of Jesus that saved her life.

As Christians, we need to remember that the law cannot redeem and free people; only our Saviour can. If we build our churches on the law, we are creating an environment of judgement and condemnation. That is not what Christ has called us to do. He said, "A new command I give you: Love one another. As I have loved you, so you must love one another" (John 13:34). All we do as the body of Christ should begin with and be driven by love. Only then are we reflecting the character of Christ and pointing people to the God who brings healing, freedom, and transformation.

Chapter Six Notes

_____

_____

_____

_____

_____

_____

_____

_____

_____

_____

_____

_____

_____

_____

_____

_____

_____

_____

_____

_____

_____

_____

CHAPTER SEVEN

Relationship Before Advice

The church functions in many ways in the lives of believers. It proclaims, instructs, guides, warns, counsels, and consoles. Relationships are woven throughout all activities held within the church's walls. Relationship is the heartbeat of the church. More importantly, it is the heartbeat of our heavenly Father. The Bible even uses marriage as a symbol of Christ and the church becoming unified as one body (Ephesians 5:28–33; 1 Corinthians 12:12–14).

As we discussed in the previous chapter, 1 Corinthians 13 reveals that love is the greatest expression of our faith. In all we do, we need to love God and love other people. First Corinthians 13 challenges us to view church structures, rules, traditions, functions, ministry programs, and positions of authority through the lens of love. There is nothing wrong with having such functions. However, people's experiences within their churches and with God can be poisoned by unhealthy fear when churches are bogged down by rigidity, power, and control and lose love as their foundation.

A Psalms Church

King David was described as a man after God's own heart (1 Samuel 13:14; Acts 13:22). In the psalms he wrote, we see a man expressing deep pain, sadness, confusion, and fear, but also one who trusts in the Lord rather than relying on his own understanding. (See Psalm 3, 4, 5, 6, 9, 11, 12, 13, 15, 18, and 19–32 as examples.)

A "Psalms church" reflects the heart of David, who experienced and expressed human weakness and suffering and chose to fall into God's arms for grace and support. This type of church is open to and equipped for the full range of human emotions in worship and counselling. A "Psalms church" also reflects the heart of God as revealed in the Psalms. There we see His zeal for justice, mercy, grace, love, forgiveness, and unity.

When we create a church that provides a haven or a hospital for hurting people, we can help them to heal. We "all have sinned and fall short of the glory of God" (Romans 3:23), so if we are honest with ourselves, we should be able to empathize with other people's faults, failures, mistakes, and shortcomings. By expressing love, being active listeners, providing warmth, validating other people's suffering, and consoling one another, we can help each other to open up, forge relationships, and mend. Our approach should be to "rejoice with those who rejoice, and weep with those who weep" (Romans 12:15 NKJV), engaging each other "with compassion, kindness, humility, gentleness and patience" (Colossians 3:12).

Through my years of working with Christians, I have heard too many stories of people feeling unheard, unseen, and unvalidated. Imagine struggling for years with something difficult and heavy in your life, and when you try to communicate what you are going through, you are flatly told that you simply need to pray and read your Bible more.

During difficult times, most people need to know that they are seen, heard, and loved by someone they trust. Our goal should be to console people with connection. This may involve praying with them and reading scriptures that bring peace to the soul, but it certainly does not mean dismissing their stories and offering spiritual disciplines as a simple solution to their deeply held pain.

DO WE REALLY CARE?

The stories of people going unnoticed by their church show that care ministries exist as a backdrop or do not exist at all. My heart breaks over the countless times people sitting on my couch have said, "No one asked how I was doing," or, "No one came to see me."

I have been told innumerable times, "If a pastor came to see me, I felt unheard and completely misunderstood. I was told that I didn't have enough faith. It seemed like I was given a cookie-cutter solution because he didn't really listen to my struggles. He speculated about a solution based on generalizations and rushing through the process, so I didn't even want to talk anymore."

If I could combine the sentiments of dozens of clients, they would say, "I went to see a church leader. I sat in his office and started to cry. I was broken, and when I began to share, the pastor didn't listen to my story. He interrupted me and didn't validate my struggle at all. He brought up the Bible to tell me what I should do differently. He cared about the Bible, but he didn't care about me. I wanted him to see me and hear me. Plus, I've already read those scriptures. I just want to be validated, known, and cared for. I felt rejected rather than accepted, because I was told that I wasn't doing the right thing. Instead of caring about me and my problem, the pastor wanted to offer a quick fix. Things aren't that simple, and now I assume that I'm not worth his time."

Although such narratives may be incomplete or one-sided accounts based on individuals' perceived experiences, we do need to examine how our approaches lead people to such perspectives. Many Christians have gone to their church first, seeking support from their leadership, but were left feeling disappointed, condemned, or upset. My clients have reported feeling worse instead of better after speaking with their church leaders. They said, "It seemed like I was just another cog in the wheel, not someone they wanted to build a relationship with." Contrast this type of interaction with the genuine care Jesus showed.

We see the power and comfort of Jesus' love when He wept over the loss of Lazarus even though He knew that He would raise His friend back to life (John 11). Jesus did not minimize anyone's suffering. He spoke words of comfort to Lazarus's sisters, Martha and Mary. Jesus wept as He grieved over the loss of His friend, expressing His deep, heartfelt sadness (John 11:35). John 11:33 tells us, "When Jesus saw her [Mary] weeping, and the Jews who had come along with her also weeping, he was deeply moved in spirit and troubled."

God has great compassion for those who are suffering: "The LORD is compassionate and gracious, slow to anger and abounding in faithful love" (Psalm 103:8 CSB). People will suppress their emotions when they feel alone and isolated, but Jesus offers us deep sympathy and empathy (Hebrews 4:14–16). As His followers, we need to do the same for other people.

CHRISTLIKE CONNECTION

The Apostle Paul wrote:

You must have the same attitude that Christ Jesus had. Though he was God, he did not think of equality with God as something to cling to. Instead, he gave up his divine privileges; he took the humble position of a slave and was born as a human being. When he appeared in human form, he humbled himself in obedience to God and died a criminal's death on a cross.
—Philippians 2:5–8 NLT

Jesus is the Son of God, but He humbly put others before Himself. His servant's heart was demonstrated to the greatest degree at the cross, where He died a shameful death that He did not deserve. Though He would be exalted and every knee would one day bow to Him (Philippians 2:9–11), He came to serve, not to be served (Mark 10:45).

Most people would be interested in meeting Jesus. Why would we want to sit down with Jesus? Because of His character. Jesus' love, grace, selflessness, and genuine care for people draw us to Him. I have heard even non-believers say that they would love to go back in time and share a meal with Jesus. When I asked why, they said, "Because He cared for people no matter where they came from. He talked with prostitutes and showed them love and compassion. He was full of gentleness, sympathy, and kindness." Shouldn't people also be able to say this of Jesus' followers?

Scripture instructs us, "Do nothing out of selfish ambition or vain conceit. Rather, in humility value others above yourselves, not looking to your own interests but each of you to the interests of the others" (Philippians 2:3–4). As the body of Christ, the hands and feet of Jesus, we must learn to serve others and genuinely care for them. We must follow the example of our Saviour by humbly putting others before ourselves.

RELATIONSHIP FIRST

People will not allow us to give them advice until we have developed trust by showing that we truly care for them in this Christlike way. Only after we have established a connection with someone and built a relationship should we give advice or share Scripture. We should not assume that we have the right to provide advice just because people show up at our door. They may not be ready to receive what we have to offer. If we have not entered into someone's life as a caring person, our counsel and sharing of Scripture will likely be ineffective.

Scripture describes how to be loving in our interactions:

> *Therefore, as God's chosen people, holy and dearly loved, clothe yourselves with compassion, kindness, humility, gentleness and patience. Bear with each other and forgive one another if any of you has a grievance against someone. Forgive as the Lord forgave you. And over all these virtues put on love, which binds them all together in perfect unity.*
> *—Colossians 3:12–14*

These are not qualities and behaviours that come to us naturally, or we would not be told to "clothe" ourselves with them. These traits are similar to the fruit of the Spirit (Galatians 5:22–23), which means that they cannot be generated apart from the power of the Holy Spirit. As we develop and display these Christlike characteristics, people will be more likely to connect with us and be vulnerable with us. This vulnerability is needed for people to share their deepest struggles and emotions. Only after the relationship has developed in this way should we impart advice.

A person came to see me because of religious-based trauma. She had PTSD from her time at a very controlling and legalistic church, and she lived in the grip of fear. I ended up working with her for a few years. It was only through the relationship we developed that she started to heal. Mind you, relationship with me is never enough. Ultimately, Jesus set her free by using me as a willing vessel to be led by His Spirit and help her toward healing.

This client said that she never felt as seen and heard as she did in our time together. When I counsel someone, all that matters is that person. There can be no distractions, no looking at a phone or a watch or even out the window. I want to be very present with the person in front of me.

She also said that it was because she was never shamed in our interactions that she was able to heal and experience God's love and freedom. I tried to show her compassion, empathy, and kindness, and she said that it was her first time being treated in this way. I wanted her to experience God's love for her through me and knew that my being a vessel for the Lord would help her to heal.

The genuine connection made all the difference. She had never experienced that before, even though she grew up in a Christian family and attended various churches throughout her life. Brené Brown, who has studied empathy and vulnerability for many years, writes, "Empathy is communicating that incredibly healing message of, 'You are not alone.'" That message is what we must communicate, both verbally and non-verbally, every time we meet with someone.

CONNECT TO YOURSELF FIRST

I think a word of caution is helpful to discuss in this context. When people come to see you, pay attention to what makes you uncomfortable. This feeling could be an indicator that you are projecting your own unresolved past onto people who are seeking your help. If you have trouble dealing with the emotions of others, it may be that you are having trouble processing your own emotions. Perhaps what the other person is sharing triggers a painful memory in you, maybe even one that you hold subconsciously.

You may try to silence the person expressing emotion by offering advice prematurely if you do not feel comfortable experiencing other people's emotions. You may be triggered by it and pull back, keeping you from following the biblical instruction to "weep with those who weep" (Romans 12:15 NKJV).

To be connected to another person, you must first be connected to yourself. Be aware of what makes you uncomfortable and use those experiences as an opportunity to learn where you may need to heal.

CONNECTION STRATEGIES

Here are some tips to help you develop a relationship before offering advice:

1. Get to know the individual in a personal way. Pray that God's love will fill your heart and overflow toward him or her.

2. Ask many open-ended questions so you can understand this person's personality, pain, and sorrow through the story he or she is telling. Your first reaction may be to try to solve rather than listen, but people seeking counsel need to be heard first.

3. Listen with great attentiveness. How would you want someone to listen to you? You would want people to look at you, be engaged, nod their heads, and be genuinely interested. So remove distractions and pay attention. Make sure that your body language communicates your attentiveness.

4. Use language of validation, such as "That must be painful," "I can see the sadness in your eyes," or "That must be really stressful for you."

5. Do not rush the process. When people want advice, they will ask for it. Take the time to build the relationship and listen for the invitation to offer counsel.

6. Be patient. Understand from the outset of the relationship that it will take a long time to build trust and for people to open up to you.

GRACE AND TRUTH

Every person who enters my office is doing or believing something that causes him or her to stumble. I cannot perceive what that is and, therefore, cannot offer help that is truly helpful until the client feels loved and validated by me. Until that person trusts me, I will sound like Charlie Brown's teacher on the intercom. This is not to minimize those who have suffered abuse or have been victims of some heinous act. My point is that any counsel I can give, even if it is sound and true, cannot be received if the person is still trapped in the fear-based responses of the soul and body that result from unresolved trauma.

The healing process will involve unlearning some false narratives, such as "I'm unlovable," that keep replaying in the person's mind as a result of the trauma. This is why understanding the interplay of grace and truth is so important. People need to hear the truth, but unless they experience grace first, they will not be able to receive the truth. We always begin with grace and follow with truth.

Sometimes people ask me, "How did you become such a good listener and so empathetic?" The answer is quite simple: I spent much of my life feeling unheard and unvalidated. Then I began to work with a few mentors who sat down with me and were willing to hear my story. They genuinely listened to me and never judged or shamed me. Through them, I saw and experienced the character of Jesus, which gave me the incentive to change my life and to give what I had received. I wanted others to experience the transformative love and grace that I had experienced.

I am reminded of what the Apostle Paul wrote in 2 Corinthians 1:3–4: "Blessed be the God and Father of our Lord Jesus Christ, the Father of mercies and the God of all comfort. He comforts us in all our affliction, so that we may be able to comfort those who are in any kind of affliction, through the comfort we ourselves receive from God" (CSB).

The love that others showed me helped me to see how God loves me, which brought about healing and transformation. Through my personal experience and what I have witnessed in my years of counselling the broken-hearted, I can attest to the deep and lasting change that occurs when Christians love one another, encourage one another, and bear one another's burdens.

Chapter Seven Notes

PART D:
Peace, Freedom, and Love—
What Healing Looks Like

CHAPTER EIGHT

Freedom in the Eye of the Storm

Freedom can be expressed in a thousand different ways according to one's dreams, hopes, and desires. If a picture is worth a thousand words, just a handful of people could express millions of words with the images of freedom in their minds. What is your picture of freedom?

People commonly desire to escape to picturesque places, where stress, injustice, and personal suffering can be paused or forgotten for a while. Freedom feels like a dream from which reality will abruptly awaken us, because this world is not our home. We are sojourners, passing through this broken and fallen world as we wait for the return of our King, who will set things right (Psalm 39:12; Psalm 119:19; Hebrews 11:9–10; 1 Peter 2:11–12; 2 Peter 3; Revelation 19–22). Yet most people, including Christians, seek healing and freedom from a world that cannot satisfy a wounded soul (John 4; 7:37–39).

FREEDOM IN CHRIST ALONE

Freedom in this world feels like a fantasy or like a lottery commercial promising autonomy, joy, and peace through materialism and wealth. The wounded and suffering soul seeks a place to rest but finds only fleeting moments of escape. Freedom is found not in this world but in the one who came to save it. Jesus Christ "was wounded for our transgressions, He was crushed for our wickedness [our sin, our injustice, our wrongdoing]; the punishment [required] for our well-being fell on Him, and by His stripes (wounds) we are healed" (Isaiah 53:5 AMP).

Only through Jesus, who died for our sins and rose from the dead, can we know the truth that will set us free (John 8:32). Galatians 5:1 tells us, "It is for freedom that Christ has set us free. Stand firm, then, and do not let yourselves be burdened again by a yoke of slavery." This freedom cannot be measured by the world's standards. It is eternal freedom for those who trust in Christ for the gift of salvation.

Some clients believe that if they are healed from the pain of past wounds, they will experience freedom. But in reality, as important as that healing may be, true freedom can come only through a relationship with Jesus Christ. Healing can come from freedom, but some people may experience a measure of healing without knowing the freedom that comes through Christ alone.

For example, someone who is not a believer may speak with me at my office about her struggles with forgiving her father. She may come to a place where she forgives her father, but that does not mean that she knows Christ, is experiencing the blessings of salvation and freedom from sin, and will go to heaven. On the other hand, someone could be bound to a wheelchair, going through tremendous struggles in her marriage, or grieving, yet live in freedom and peace because she knows Jesus Christ.

FREEDOM AND DISCIPLESHIP

How can believers experience freedom in Jesus Christ as we sojourn in this world? How do we fulfill the mission to "make disciples of all nations" (Matthew 28:18–20) while not being stained by the sins of the world?

Billy Graham lived a life testifying to the love of Jesus Christ. His reputation as a faithful disciple of Christ was known around the world. In his devotional, Graham stated:
[35]

> The mark of a true Christian is found in his personal relationship to the Person of Jesus Christ. Christianity is Christ. Christ is Christianity. I speak reverently when I say that Jesus is more than His ideas. All that He said was true, but without Him even the truth would have been powerless. Men know the power of truth, and truth is that which sets men free. Jesus said, "I am the truth."

The truth that sets us free is found in the person of Jesus Christ. When Jesus preached in a synagogue in Nazareth, He unrolled the scroll and chose to speak from Isaiah 61 (Luke 4:16–17). He declared, "The Spirit of the Lord is on me, because he has anointed me to proclaim good news to the poor. He has sent me to proclaim freedom for the prisoners and recovery of sight for the blind, to set the oppressed free, to proclaim the year of the Lord's favor" (Luke 4:18–19). Part of Jesus' mission is to set people free through the blood He shed on the cross for our eternal salvation.

ABIDE IN CHRIST

Connecting with Christ's heart is foundational to healing the human spirit, soul, and body. Only by being yoked to Christ can our souls find rest (Matthew 11:28–30). In earlier chapters, we saw that the key to holistic healing of our tripartite being is establishing caring relationships through humility and empathy. These relationships must be based on love and truth. However, we cannot sustain connection with and empathy for others who are broken and wounded if we do not remain close to Jesus ourselves.

We know that the Scriptures tell us to remove the planks from our own eyes before trying to help other people with their problems (Matthew 7:3–5). Every wounded soul can project hurt onto another person, whether subconsciously or consciously. One person's hurt converges with another's, which leads to disunity. Every person wants to be received like the prodigal son, with open arms and no judgement (Luke 15:11–32). However, this is only possible in a church where believers stay connected to Christ so they can be developing Christlike character:

126

I am the true vine, and my Father is the gardener. He cuts off every branch in me that bears no fruit, while every branch that does bear fruit he prunes so that it will be even more fruitful. You are already clean because of the word I have spoken to you. Remain in me, as I also remain in you. No branch can bear fruit by itself; it must remain in the vine. Neither can you bear fruit unless you remain in me.

I am the vine; you are the branches. If you remain in me and I in you, you will bear much fruit; apart from me you can do nothing. If you do not remain in me, you are like a branch that is thrown away and withers; such branches are picked up, thrown into the fire and burned. If you remain in me and my words remain in you, ask whatever you wish, and it will be done for you. This is to my Father's glory, that you bear much fruit, showing yourselves to be my disciples.

As the Father has loved me, so have I loved you. Now remain in my love. If you keep my commands, you will remain in my love, just as I have kept my Father's commands and remain in his love. I have told you this so that my joy may be in you and that your joy may be complete. My command is this: Love each other as I have loved you.
—John 15:1–12

For every person, freedom and peace come from being and remaining connected to Jesus in a loving relationship.

BEYOND FACTS

We need to know Jesus beyond religious facts and logic. We need to know and hold His love in our spirits, souls, and bodies to the point that we cannot conceive of a life without Him. I remember the day that Jesus pierced my heart. I was twelve years old and attending a Christian camp called

Braeside. Church was foundational to my family, but religion and Jesus became very different for me that night.

Though Jesus saved me at that camp, I did not yet have the biblical knowledge to understand what had happened. All I knew was that I had experienced Jesus in a real and personal way. I knew that the Spirit of the living God had transformed me through salvation in Jesus Christ. I experienced the love of Jesus as the Holy Spirit fell upon me. His love was and continues to be immeasurable.

I felt a profound peace and freedom. I remember feeling as though my feet were walking on a cloud, and I skipped all the way back to my cabin, singing childhood praises to the Lord. My life was changed forever.

This also meant that Satan was ready "to steal and kill and destroy" (John 10:10). I spent many years walking through various trials and tribulations, as Jesus told us we would (John 16:33), such as being bullied and hiding in a bathroom, an abusive Christian marriage, divorce, remarriage, and my oldest child being diagnosed with and battling cancer for seven years. My faith wavered because I did not yet know my identity in Christ.

SURRENDER BRINGS FREEDOM

Only after the relapse of my son's cancer did I surrender my entire spirit, soul, and body to Jesus while weeping over the kitchen table for hours. It was then that I received the revelation that I was a blood-bought child of God, and I experienced "the peace of God, which surpasses all understanding" (Philippians 4:7 NKJV). Jesus became my everything, and I wanted to know how to be His hands and feet to anyone the Lord sent across my path. This meant that I needed to learn and continually relearn how to love others as Christ loves the church, even when I am betrayed, battered, and rejected.

Freedom comes when our identity in Jesus Christ does not unravel at the first sign of a threat. Though often an unpleasant journey, the sanctified life is critical. As we experience the "refiner's fire" over and over again, dross is removed (Malachi 3:2–3). This purification process allows for the development of Christlike character that enables us to walk toward people with open arms, demonstrating the heart of Christ to a lost world, even when there is a risk of rejection and abandonment. We learn to stand with the whole armour of God (Ephesians 6:10–17), instead of the fear-based strategies of the brain, as our protection, knowing that our Lord will never forsake us (Deuteronomy 31:6).

Some people have shared with me that religion felt like imprisonment. They attended a legalistic church, where bondage and heaviness caused them to be trapped in fear to the point of despair. This environment does not reflect the character of Christ, who said, "Peace I leave with you; my peace I give you. I do not give to you as the world gives. Do not let your hearts be troubled and do not be afraid" (John 14:27). Religion imprisons, but Jesus gives freedom and peace.

POLYVAGAL THEORY

Neuroscience has shown us that steps can be taken to help people if something within their bodies is preventing them from experiencing this freedom and peace. For instance, someone who is saved may still be struggling with a past traumatic experience. In the past, counsellors focused on helping the person with this logically, emphasizing cognitive issues, but these methods may not result in the client actually feeling and living from a place of peace. When we understand the human nervous system and recognize that it discharges fear, we can engage it to remove tension, stress, and anxiety. This is called *polyvagal theory*.[36]

Everyone's nervous system holds a story. Because this part of the body can hold the effects of a painful experience, we cannot always talk and reason ourselves out of the pain or the wound. We must experience a change physically through various techniques, such as EMDR, to bring about complete healing.

I helped one client who had suffered from sexual abuse and was undergoing cognitive behaviour therapy for over ten years but had never experienced freedom or peace. I assisted her in feeling the trauma so that she could release it. She needed to experience the pain to let it go. You must permit your body to feel the pain. When we are too logical, we ignore or suppress the nervous system, allowing it to continue in its current patterns. However, when we engage the body as well as the soul, the nervous system can release the pain and free the body from specific memories or triggers.

EMBRACE YOUR IDENTITY IN CHRIST

When we embrace our identity in Jesus, we can meet people where they are and demonstrate genuine empathy. We are able to be vulnerable with other people, which encourages them to do the same with us. Vulnerability is the opposite of fear. Counsellors need to create a safe environment so that clients can become vulnerable, which is the first step toward accessing freedom and experiencing peace. Brené Brown describes the complex role of vulnerability as follows: "vulnerability is the core of shame and fear and our struggle for worthiness, but it appears that it is also the birthplace of joy, of creativity, of belonging, of love."[37]

People have told me countless times that Christians should not need a therapist. They believe that seeking this type of counsel sends the signal that their faith, their God, their pastor, and their church community are somehow deficient. This mindset does not reflect the will of God, who does not condemn us for seeking help, especially through counsellors that He has gifted. God meets us exactly where we are to bring healing so that we can know the peace that is found in Jesus Christ.

This healing from our heavenly Father does not always come overnight. Though God is capable of instantaneous healing, He often takes people along an unexpected path. When people do not experience healing in the way and the timing they are hoping for, they may become discouraged and start to lose faith in the character of God and His love for them. We need to understand that our heavenly Father is with us in our pain and on every step of the journey toward healing. He may give us access to forms of healing that we do not expect, and we need to surrender to His sovereignty, allowing the path on which He takes each of us to give us greater insight into who He is and who we are in Christ.

I always encourage people to look to the Father as He unfolds a story of beauty that comes from walking with Him, wherever He will lead us. The unfolding stories of our unique paths to healing are meant to be shared. These stories have great value when we offer them as a testimony to God's love, faithfulness, grace, and power and to encourage one another and build each other up in Christ, for the glory of God.

We need to be grounded in the love of Christ to experience the kind of freedom that enables us to love and serve others. I often say that freedom feels like sitting with Jesus in the eye of the storm, where it is calm and peaceful, as the chaos swirls around us. We all want this type of freedom, but it comes at a cost. We must lay down our lives (Matthew 16:24–25; 1 John 3:16) and crucify our flesh (Romans 8:13; Galatians 2:20) so that we can be used by God for His purposes.

When we submit to God and adopt this posture of self-sacrificial obedience, choosing to find our identity in Christ above all else, He will use us as part of the fulfillment of this prayer: "Our Father in heaven, hallowed be your name, your kingdom come, your will be done, on earth as it is in heaven" (Matthew 6:9–10). Religious acts and recitation have led to spiritual amnesia. We have forgotten that "God did not send his Son into the world to condemn the world, but to save the world through him" (John 3:17). Let us bring the kingdom of God down together by first looking in the mirror. As the old hymn says:[38]

> There's a dawn arising on a brand-new day
>
> There's a strong wind stirring 'cross the ancient graves
>
> There's a voice that's calling, "Will you be set free?"
>
> There's a change a-coming
>
> Let it start in me.

Chapter Eight Notes

_____

_____

_____

_____

_____

_____

_____

_____

_____

_____

_____

_____

_____

_____

_____

_____

_____

_____

_____

_____

Are You a Free or Shackled Leader?

A pastor once came to see me because he was concerned that he was going to burn out. Though he had pastored his large church for many years, he was dealing with a tremendous amount of pain and conflict among the staff and congregation. He had positioned people in leadership who had ended up causing conflicts and division. These same leaders even questioned his character, ministry, and staffing decisions. This pastor stopped realizing that he had to make hard decisions. Not surprisingly, all that was happening with the leadership had a ripple effect in the congregation.

All these issues plagued him and caused him to question his own worth and identity as a Christian and a pastor. They also stirred up painful memories of parental abandonment from when he was a teenager. In fact, during this difficult time in the pastorate, many other wounds from his past resurfaced, bringing feelings of blame, shame, brokenness, and rejection. His unresolved wounds led him to feel past pain in his current situation.

It is important to note that this pastor believed in, relied on, and knew Scripture. In fact, that was how he knew that something was off. He knew that his ministry should not feel like a painful burden that was weighing him down beyond what he could bear.

Over time, we developed trust, and he began to open up about his life. I told him to put down his pastor's hat and allow himself to be real with me, reassuring him that it was okay not to have everything together. I needed to create a safe space and give him permission to put down his defenses. Then it became clear that he had unresolved issues in his past that needed to be dealt with.

Both leaders and congregants need to understand that being a pastor does not mean that you are immune to wounds and unresolved issues. Many Christian leaders carry burdens and try to soldier on in their ministries. What is often overlooked is that others are impacted by this burden as well, resulting in the convergence of hurting people.

PROTECTIVE BARRIERS

If you are in a position of leadership, you are going to face turmoil from many directions: from people on your board, from other leaders, and from your congregation. People are always going to struggle with changes and shifts in decision-making. If you are not grounded and healed, the difficulties and turmoil will shake every part of you as well as impact those you are trying to help and serve.

Scripture tells us that when we are struggling with someone, we should go to that person directly and talk about our grievances. If the person will not listen to us, we are to take one or two other people along with us to discuss the problem again (Matthew 18:15–16). We are called to walk in the fruit of the Spirit, approaching people with love, patience, and kindness. Why, then, is there so much dissension and lack of hearing in church settings? Sometimes the problem is with the one who needs to hear, but often it is a convergence of two people who have unresolved issues in their lives: the person approaching and the person hearing.

The bottom line is that if leaders are not exemplifying the fruit of the Spirit, then there is something in their lives that needs pruning. And what often needs to be pruned is the wounds from the past that have never been addressed and released.

If you are a pastor or other church leader and you are hurting from unresolved painful experiences, then you will not be the only person who feels the effects of your pain. When someone else in the church—someone else in leadership, someone in your congregation, or someone in your ministry—comes to you with his or her own brokenness and perceptions, they will converge with yours, resulting in conflict and fractures in the relationship.

Instead of dealing properly with these issues, you have created protective barriers that, in the end, hurt other people as well as yourself. When you have layers upon layers of unresolved wounds, you cannot walk in the fruit of the Spirit. These layers can lead to pride and arrogance, which hinder you from leading with humility.

Does that mean that pastors and other Christian leaders can never experience wounds? No, of course not. It is the unresolved hurts and trauma that create a protective barrier and impede your ability to walk and lead in a healthy way. If you are approaching relational situations with the fruit of the Spirit, you will be able to say, "We have differences of opinion, but I love you and respect your opinion. We are going to be okay and work this problem out." Your past hurts are not shackling you, so you are able to walk with Christlike love and not allow difficulties to damage your relationship.

However, if you have unresolved hurt or trauma, it can be triggered by a present problem or struggle. Then you may become combative or walk away from the individual or problem, perhaps even leave that church, instead of coming together with the other person and working it out. The present grievances trigger the past unresolved conflicts. Layers upon layers of unresolved wounds will prevent you from handling conflict according to the fruit of the Spirit.

Do you see the cycle at play here? If people have too much unresolved hurt, it makes it difficult to approach other people from a place of humility. Though it pains me to say it, we have a lot of pride and arrogance in our churches and ministries today because too many Christian leaders think that everybody else has it wrong when the truth is that they are not leading from a right place within themselves.

People in church leadership who cannot stand in a place of boundaries and lead with grace, mercy, and the fruit of the Spirit will struggle to engage other people with Christlike humility, and their congregation and ministries will suffer the consequences. Leaders should not pretend that they have it all together. Instead, they should lead in humility, showing vulnerability and meekness as they face situations and problems from a healthy position of grace and faith.

THE RIPPLE EFFECT OF BROKEN LEADERS

My couch holds the stories of many hurting and broken people from all walks of life—parents who have lost a child, couples devasted by affairs, individuals who have suffered abuse, the loss of a parent, a job loss or transition, family conflict, and many other hardships that have and will continue to afflict all people on this earth. The faces I see in my office are worn and hopeless, yet they are still seeking restoration and the remembrance of the joy of the Lord.

James 1:2–4 says, "Consider it a great joy, my brothers and sisters, whenever you experience various trials, because you know that the testing of your faith produces endurance. And let endurance have its full effect, so that you may be mature and complete, lacking nothing" (CSB).

Every Christian must walk through the process of sanctification, being tested and refined so that he or she may more clearly reflect the light of Jesus. No follower of Christ is exempt from this process. We are all called to stay connected to Jesus, as the vine, and undergo our heavenly Father's pruning so that we will produce the fruit of the Spirit (John 15:1–17). If leaders exclude themselves from this process, believing or pretending that they do not need it, there will be a ripple effect in the people they are called to lead and influence.

THE BURDEN OF LEADERSHIP

I have observed the burden that leaders carry as they seek to edify and challenge congregants, staff, and volunteers. This burden can become overwhelmingly heavy under the weight of the leaders' own unresolved wounds that are dormant or hidden. I have heard leaders express how they had reached the point of wanting to throw it all away for a so-called "simpler life" marked by caring less for the problems of others and having decreased decision-making responsibilities.

Leadership is fueled by connection and relationship within the hierarchy of decision-making. It is important to understand that leaders are not burdened by the practical tasks of leadership, but by the triggers associated with people being disappointed, lashing out, or having misperceptions. In other words, leaders, like all other people, are hurt when others do not see, hear, and understand them. These experiences trigger reactions to painful memories and unresolved wounds.

Whether or not you are a leader, if your reactions do not match the circumstance, it reveals something connected to an unresolved wound within you. This wound might have been from rejection, betrayal, or abuse, and it goes deeper than what you are addressing in the present moment.

CONNECTING THE DOTS IN YOUR LIFE

When new clients come to their first counselling session with me, they do not say, "I've got a lot of unresolved issues from my past that I need to work on." Instead, they say, "I am having struggles in my marriage and my family. I'm having difficulties with people in my church. Right now, I'm mad at everyone!"

What is profoundly interesting in these counselling sessions is that even though the clients come to me with present-day troubles, they inevitably go back to their past. In the course of sharing what is going on in their lives, they will say, "I can remember a time when I was a child and the same thing happened."

It often takes time for people to connect the dots regarding what is really going on in their lives. They think that their problem is a certain person or situation in the present, but that is merely a trigger. The real issue is the compounding layers of past hurt and trauma that have never been resolved. The present problem is merely the mechanism that brings the genuine issues to the surface.

You need to ask yourself, "Is my present problem the real issue, or is it merely a reminder of past hurt that I have never resolved?" If you are reacting to people and situations in a way that does not demonstrate the fruit of the Spirit and you are experiencing continued strife in your personal and professional relationships, I suggest that you take time to connect the dots in your life. Then start peeling back the layers within you so you can resolve the deeper wounds that are at the core of your problems.

Jesus talked a great deal about hurt, anger, and reconciliation. He said, "Therefore, if you are offering your gift at the altar and there remember that your brother or sister has something against you, leave your gift there in front of the altar. First go and be reconciled to them; then come and offer your gift. Settle matters quickly with your adversary..." (Matthew 5:23–25). This also applies if you have something against another person.

When you do not settle matters quickly with other people, you end up imprisoned. Unresolved hurt and anger result in bitterness and a hardened heart. Instead of leading from a position of freedom, you are chained to the wounds of your past, which impedes your ability to love and shepherd the people you have been called to lead. It is time to unlock the shackles in your life. God calls you to freedom.

BREAKING THE CYCLE OF NEGATIVE PATTERNS

Something interesting happens when you start to connect the dots in your life. You will notice a pattern of behaviour—whether it is how you think, what you say, or how you act—when someone or something triggers you.

Though we can all experience triggers and the reactions they bring, it is the cycle of negative patterns developed over a lifetime that impedes our ability to have healthy relationships and lead from a place of freedom. Every time an interaction happens that reminds you of a person or experience that hurt you deeply, you respond with a strategy your brain has developed to protect you from being hurt again. This strategy can take on different forms depending on what keeps you feeling safe and in control, often by keeping other people at arm's length.

For example, you may start to notice that you always have a strong reaction to the type of personality that is direct and overbearing and asks a lot of questions. When facing someone who behaves in this way, no matter who the particular individual is, you may feel insecure and start questioning and doubting yourself. That is a pattern.

Where do these negative patterns come from? They are the result of unresolved hurt and deep wounds experienced earlier in your life. It is imperative that you become aware of your negative relationship patterns so that you can peel back the layers of your hurt and find healing, forgiveness, and freedom.

Identify Your Negative Relationship Patterns

I tell my clients to get a journal and log everything that causes them to feel that something is not right. For example, what kind of person triggers strong reactions? Taking note of these reactions can reveal patterns over time.

Perhaps someone makes you feel insecure and anxious, causing you to doubt yourself. Write it down. Is there a pattern of feeling overwhelmed and stressed around certain people?

Look for negative patterns that are connected to certain people and their behaviour. If someone's tone or facial expression bothers you, why does that impact you so strongly? If someone's mannerisms bother you, why is that? Why does it bother you when someone challenges you or does not listen to you?

When you log all these experiences and observations, your eyes will start to see the negative patterns in your life. Time and again, I have had clients do this exercise, and it has been life-changing for them. I encourage you to do the same.

Build a Timeline

Now that you have taken note of your triggers and your reactions and have identified negative patterns, the next helpful thing to do is to create a timeline of your life. Start from the very beginning—for example, your first memories of interactions with your parents and what you observed about their relationship. Then write down your experiences with your siblings, teachers, peers, and friends from your early years. After that, move on to your experiences in dating and the relationships you have had as an adult. Include your bosses and co-workers as well.

The point of the timeline is to determine the origin of your pain and how these wounds caused negative patterns of feelings, thoughts, and responses in your personal relationships. Connect the dots in your life and reflect on the experience that is causing the trigger. Write down the painful memory that comes up when you are reacting strongly to someone in the present.

When you connect the dots, become aware of your

negative patterns, and then pinpoint where in your life these patterns started, it will open your eyes to the weight you have been carrying. You will understand that you are dealing not only with someone in the present moment, but with someone in your past as well.

Challenge Your Patterns

The final step in this process is to find facts to disprove or challenge your negative patterns. It is important to identify what you can do to stop the cycle. As we discussed at the beginning of this book, it is possible to change your patterns. Once you identify your negative patterns, you can begin replacing them with healthy ones.

If talking with an aggressive person leads you to complain about that person to someone else or talk negatively about yourself, you can choose instead to pray for the aggressive person. Find scriptures that counter your negative self-talk with how God sees you and describes you. Every time you speak to someone who is aggressive and it causes you to have self-doubt and think that you are not good enough, ask yourself what the Bible says about you.

In order to change our patterns, we need to pause long enough to notice our thoughts, emotions, and behaviours. I am not suggesting that the other individuals involved should not do the same, but we are called not to cast the first stone. We need to be aware of ourselves and lead people to change by being an example first and then, when invited, speaking the truth in love. We can change an environment and interaction pattern only if we first examine ourselves.

There may be people with whom you need to establish boundaries, but if you cannot respond in love through your boundaries, it is time to ask yourself why. Remember that your true struggle is not with the person who triggers you in the present, but rather with your hurt from the past that you have not yet addressed.

If you are trying to make changes in your life by renewing your mind but it feels like you are running into a brick wall with the above approach, then it may help to change to a bottom-up approach using a method like EMDR, with a trained professional. Once you find the story held in your brain and nervous system, your thoughts (prefrontal cortex) can shift to receive new beliefs. In this way, you can unlearn your negative relationship patterns and replace them with healthy, biblical patterns. Your heavenly Father will meet you where you are and help you through this process, never shaming or condemning you.

VULNERABILITY IN LEADERSHIP

After extensive research on shame, vulnerability, and leadership, including conducting interviews and creating cognitive instruments, Brené Brown summarized her findings in her book *Dare to Lead*.[39] Her summary includes three key points to help all leaders.

Her first point is that "you can't get to courage without rumbling with vulnerability." She describes a *rumble* as "a discussion, conversation, or meeting defined by commitment to lean into vulnerability; to stay curious and generous, to stick with the messy middle of the problem." *Rumbling* is also a matter of "identification and solving" that may require a leader to "take a break and circle back when necessary, to be fearless in owning our parts, and, as psychologist Harriet Lerner teaches, to listen with the same passion with which we want to be heard."

Brown's second point is that leaders need "self-awareness and self-love. Who we are is how we lead." Lastly, she states, "Courage is contagious. To scale daring leadership and build courage in teams and organizations, we must cultivate a culture in which brave work, tough conversations, and whole hearts are the expectation, and armor is not necessary or rewarded."

We need to understand that courage and vulnerability walk hand in hand. Leaders must be willing and equipped to engage in difficult, open conversations with people. In order to promote an environment of vulnerability, they must first demonstrate vulnerability themselves.

Every person develops armour to keep him or her safe from harm. These rigid, protective structures contain thoughts, emotions, and behaviours that keep other people at arm's length. Armour is the opposite of vulnerability. Unresolved past wounds of abandonment, rejection, and betrayal lead people to develop protective strategies to ensure that their wounds are covered and to keep themselves from being hurt again.

Leaders who stay behind their armour keep other people at a distance, which causes a cyclical experience of wounding oneself and others. We have learned through the course of this book that we heal wounds through vulnerability and connection. It may be helpful to remember the following adage: "Trauma teaches you to close your heart and armor up. Healing teaches you to open your heart and boundary up."[40]

Peter Scazzero, in his book *The Emotionally Healthy Leader*, describes an emotionally unhealthy leader "as someone who operates in a continuous state of emotional and spiritual deficit, lacking emotional maturity and a 'being with God' sufficiency to sustain their 'doing for God.'" He adds, "Unhealthy leaders lack, for example, awareness of their feelings, their weaknesses and limits, and how their past impacts their present, and how others experience them."[41]

We have discussed the ripple effect of a leader's unresolved wounds, but the same is true of healing. If you are in a position of leadership, the healing of your own spirit, soul, and body will serve to draw your team and your church to greater transformation. God calls every believer to seek intimacy with Him before and above all else. He is not asking us to figure this out overnight, but to engage in a journey of transformation that is possible only if we seek to surrender to the process of change. We also have the indwelling of the Holy Spirit, who desires to guide us to healing, wisdom, and peace beyond our understanding.

WIRED TO HEAL

Leaders of all stripes have come to my office with stories of compassion fatigue, stress, and burnout. These present-day stories have an organic way of leading people to their wounds from the past. As a therapist, I have witnessed courageous leaders step into a place of discomfort as they share painful stories burdened with concealed shame.

If you were to sit on my couch, I am confident that you would hear me say, "Our past informs our present and determines our future." This does not mean that we are doomed to a particular future because of what we already experienced in the past. We can now find great hope in this statement because we have come to see that we are wired to heal.

My greatest challenge to you is to be willing to go to the places in your past that are difficult to revisit, because doing so will draw you to deep healing and an intimate experience with Jesus. In this place of intimacy with your Saviour, freedom will finally prevail as you come to the understanding that you cannot earn your way to Jesus. He did everything for you at Calvary. All you have to do is submit yourself and your life to Him.

THE WEIGHT OF EXPECTATIONS

Many leaders become focused on the daily tasks of decision-making, building, and organizing. They spend little time in Sabbath rest and intimate worship of the Lord. As a result, fatigue, stress, and burnout compound the unresolved wounds, causing increasing numbers of Christian leaders to suffer from depression, leave their positions, or even commit suicide. Though we see the rise in mental illness, if we do not understand how the integration of neuroscience and

Scripture can break the silence and bring healing, we will remain stuck in unhealthy patterns that can produce devastating consequences.

We need leaders to engage in transforming their inner lives, speak out with vulnerability, and lead with courage. Andrew Stoecklein, a pastor of a megachurch and a mental health advocate, took his life a few years ago. Commenting on this, Ed Stetzer, a well-known Christian leader and the Director of the Billy Graham Center at Wheaton College, was concerned that unrealistic expectations are foisted upon pastors. He said, "Pastors are supposed to provide help, not need help. Pastors are supposed to speak of life, not despair. But that's not reality."[42]

The California pastor had the boldness to break walls of shame and speak forth in vulnerability, but in the end, he was overcome by his own suffering. This pastor's suicide speaks to the continued need to have conversations and sermons concerning mental health. We need to understand that anyone can succumb to pain and suffering. Leaders are not exempt from the burdens and struggles that other people experience, and their position adds the overwhelming weight of unrealistic expectations.

The misguided perception that pastors and other Christian leaders are required to have it all together has caused many of them to hide their pain in silence, where it cannot be healed. I recall many stories of Christian leaders stuck in childhood wounds of a parent leaving or of abuse, which led to drugs, alcohol, and sex in their teenage years. The guilt and shame, often deeply rooted and unacknowledged, continued

150

to poison their existence, and they eventually reached the point of being ready to give up their position and ministry. It was through my own experience of Jesus' loving embrace that I could empathize, comfort, and pour out God's living water to these hurting leaders.

FREE TO LEAD

Jesus calls each of us to embrace Him, which brings a remedy to all our guilt, shame, and sorrow. Our Father in heaven uses us as His vessels, filling us up and pouring us out to others. But before we can pour out compassion and unconditional love, we must receive them. We cannot serve perfectly, but if we receive Jesus' perfect love, we will be able to offer grace and mercy to other people. Leaders need to begin with their own healing and stay connected to Jesus so they can pour out all that God gives them with courageous vulnerability.

My greatest desire is for everyone to understand how the interwoven nature of the human spirit, soul, and body shapes the way we perceive ourselves and experience relationships so that we can first address our own wounds and then help others to find healing. We must engage in this transformative process as individuals, but never alone. We do life together. We heal through connection and in relationship with each other. This is how our heavenly Father designed us. A vulnerable relationship rooted in love is the key that unlocks healing, and healing breaks off the shackles so we can lead from a position of freedom.

Chapter Nine Notes

Love Is Foundational

If you were to walk down the stairs to my family room, you would see a scripture hanging on the wall as a reminder that love "bears all things, believes all things, hopes all things, endures all things" (1 Corinthians 13:7 NKJV).

Whenever I read that scripture, I like to think of the Amplified Bible version: "Love bears all things [regardless of what comes], believes all things [looking for the best in each one], hopes all things [remaining steadfast during difficult times], endures all things [without weakening]" (1 Corinthians 13:7 AMP).

LOVE IS AN ACTION

In a family that experiences heartache, sorrow, and pain in equal measure with joy and happiness, is this a difficult task? Of course, it is. Love is a choice that we make each day; it is not based on a fleeting emotion. Love is laying down your life for another. Love is Jesus, who laid down His life for us at the cross. As we read in 1 John 3:16, "This is how we know what love is: Jesus Christ laid down his life for us. And we ought to lay down our lives for our brothers and sisters."

In the Bible, love is described more often as a commitment or action than as a mere emotion. Look again at 1 Corinthians 13 and you will see that love is described in terms that take effort, intentionality, commitment, and the leading of the Holy Spirit. Throughout this book, there has been a view of integrating science and the Bible to understand how people suffer, transform, and heal. Our discussion has shown that science glorifies God and that expanding our awareness of the complex and interwoven nature of the spirit, soul, and body will help us to meet people exactly where they are and listen to their deeply held stories, without judgement.

My challenge to you as you read this final chapter is to view this as the most important chapter, because if we do not learn how to love well, then everything else in this book will come to nothing. The Apostle Paul wrote, "And if I have the gift of prophecy [and speak a new message from God to the people], and understand all mysteries, and [possess] all knowledge; and if I have all [sufficient] faith so that I can remove mountains, but do not have love [reaching out to others], I am nothing" (1 Corinthians 13:2 AMP). Relationships based on the love of Christ are the context in which healing and transformation occur.

TRUSTING JESUS' PERFECT LOVE

How do we apply the knowledge and wisdom of an integrated view of science and the word of God if we do not first love God supremely and love our neighbours as ourselves? We cannot truly help suffering people if we do not love them as Christ loves the church.

In my younger years, a haunting reflection of myself stared back at me, filled with insecurity and rejection. Throughout my twenties and thirties, I saw the world through my own unresolved wounds. I stayed guarded and lived behind a metaphorical wall. The eyes that looked at me in the mirror were the same eyes that looked at others with fear. Our fears prevent us from walking alongside others who are imprisoned in their own pain. However, when we know the truth of Jesus' love for us and are open to receiving it, we can see a reflection of Jesus looking back at us, with eyes full of mercy and grace.

We can extend grace to others when we remember the grace that was demonstrated for us at the cross. I could extend love when I felt confident that I would not be hurt in return. It was not that I believed that other people would love me perfectly; it was that I knew and trusted Jesus' perfect love for me. Love takes courage and vulnerability. The more I rested in God's love, the more often I could extend love to others, no matter the risk.

When I was in my thirties, I came across a C. S. Lewis quote from *The Four Loves* that gripped my heart. He stated, "To love at all is to be vulnerable" and risk your heart breaking. But the alternative, Lewis wrote, is to lock up your heart so that it becomes "unbreakable, impenetrable, irredeemable."

I did not want to lay lifeless or numb in a casket of my own making. This meant that I had to take the risk and choose vulnerability, which required looking into my brokenness and wounds from the past so I could learn how to love authentically, with honour and respect.

The most genuine expression of love starts with the revelation of how much Jesus loves us. Then we can extend the type of love revealed in 1 Corinthians 13 to others. I am not exempt from a journey of healing and sanctification. I have experienced the effects of a wall first-hand, both personally and professionally.

FROM REJECTION CAME MY STORY

When I was a child, I was very shy. It took me a long time to find my voice. I then became opinionated and argued quite a bit with my mother. We both had strong personalities and were often in conflict with one another. She and I clashed about so many things as I was growing up.

When I was about thirteen years old, I told my mom—rudely and with disrespect—how much she had hurt my feelings. What I said was harsh but true. As she walked out of my room, she looked at me with a furious, disapproving facial expression and said, "Tina, I wash my hands of you." At that moment, rejection became my story.

I was devastated. It felt as if she had permanently rejected me. I then built a giant wall to keep people at a distance, because I believed that I was unworthy. I lived behind this wall for years. My mother's words made me feel as small as a grain of sand. When a friend no longer wants to be friends with you, that is one thing. But when the person who is supposed to love you unconditionally says, "I'm done with you," that is another matter entirely.

It is difficult to find a way to express how deeply that wounded me and how hard it was to get over those stinging words. To think that the woman who gave birth to me would want nothing to do with me made me feel like a crumpled-up piece of paper discarded in a garbage can. After my mother said those words, I ran down the road in absolute pain, completely shattered inside. My father drove after me and told me to get in the car and come back home. That did not fix what my mom had said, and it took me many years to heal.

Looking back, I understand that my mom was parenting from unresolved trauma and wounds from her past. When I expressed with words of disrespect how she had hurt me, she viewed my words through her own trauma lens. Her story was triggered, so she subconsciously rejected me from behind her wall of protection. But at the time, I could not see any of this. My brain was not fully developed, and I was unaware of my mom's story until later in life.

The pain of rejection led me to make many unhealthy choices down the road. That said, I do not want to imply that I am blaming my mom for my choices. My choices, though motivated by the pain of rejection, were entirely my own.

Unresolved wounds in you can wound another person

deeply. Hurt people hurt people. I am glad to say that my mother and I now have a great relationship, but it took many years of working through various issues and practicing much of what I have shared in the previous pages to get to that place. Today, my mom is one of my greatest spiritual mentors, intercessors, encouragers, and supporters. Jesus healed us from the inside out. He gave me a new lens of appreciation and honour toward my mom, who holds a beautiful story of Jesus' love enveloping her. I could not be more blessed to have been given her as my mom.

DESIGNED TO BE LOVED

Fear of rejection and abandonment drives us to build walls of protection in our lives. We find ways to conceal and distract ourselves in an attempt to avoid further pain. Walls are the opposite of love. We cannot build connections with other people from behind our walls. This was my story until Jesus overwhelmed my heart and enabled me to see my own pain through the eyes of His grace and forgiveness. The world needs to see these same eyes through us as we reflect Jesus' love for the broken-hearted.

When we understand our identity in Christ, we can capture the essence of His love and pour it out to other people. We often hear this sentiment in Christian circles but forget that love is the foundation of helping, empathy, vulnerability, connection, and healthy relationships. The most important thing that we can do as Christians is to love like Jesus "first loved us" (1 John 4:19). His "perfect love drives out fear" (1 John 4:18) and is the basis for lasting transformation of people, relationships, and the church.

In a book entitled *Born for Love*, Bruce Perry, M.D., Ph.D., and Maia Szalavitz point out the role of early experiences in our development of the ability to love:[43]

> We are indeed born for love. But at birth, we are not yet fully loving. Infants' brains are the most malleable—and vulnerable—that they will ever be outside the womb. The gifts of our biology are a potential, not a guarantee. And with so many other human potentials present at birth, empathy and love require specific experiences to develop. Just as Mozart could never have become a musical genius if his father hadn't provided lessons and instruments—and Michael Jordan would not have become the superb athlete he has been without access to hoops, balls, and courts—babies don't learn to care and connect without specific early experience.

Babies need someone to take care of them and love them. Our biological makeup shows that we are designed to be loved. If we do not experience the love that is necessary, we become unhealthy, both physically and emotionally. Perry and Szalavitz have seen this first-hand through their work in orphanages.

They provide further insight regarding our development of the ability to love:[44]

> Consequently, while we are born for love, we need to receive it in certain ways early in life to benefit from its mercy. We need to practice love as we grow through different social experiences to best be able to give it back in

159

abundance. The brain becomes what it does frequently. It is shaped every day by what we do—and what we don't do.

In his best-selling book about his work with maltreated children, *The Boy Who Was Raised as a Dog*, Dr. Perry recounts stories of traumatized children and the impact on brain development. He speaks about the neuroscience of trauma on the brain and explains that healing for those who have experienced trauma occurs through the experiences of empathy, connection, healthy relationships, and, most importantly, love. Dr. Perry writes:[45]

> Ultimately, what determines how children survive trauma, physically, emotionally, or psychologically, is whether the people around them—particularly the adults they should be able to trust and rely upon—stand by them with love, support, and encouragement.

Throughout my work in mental health, I have come to understand that no treatment modality, scientific method, or even biblical scripture will truly change a human being if we do not lead with love. One study reported by Sharpley, Jeffrey, and McMah stated that over 80% of positive therapy outcomes may result from the therapeutic relationship in which the therapist exhibits warmth, empathy, and respect for the client.[46]

It does not matter how much scientific or biblical knowledge you have or how many books you have read. If you do not love people, none of that will help. I encourage people to learn more about neuroscience and the areas of counselling I am passionate about, but I also know that if we do not love people, they will never heal.

SIT BEHIND ANOTHER'S WALL

Many clients come to me with fear of being rejected based on their past. I speak with people coming out of difficult situations in foster care or who have been sexually abused. They believe that they are safe only behind their walls. However, if someone sees and accepts them as they are, they are willing to open up.

This is not about breaking down people's walls. We need to listen to people's stories without judgement and earn their trust so that they will invite us to sit with them behind their walls. Then we get the privilege of helping them to remove those bricks, one by one, from the inside. In my experience, when I meet clients where they are and sit with them behind their walls so they know that I care for them unconditionally, this often leads to breakthroughs and healthy transformation.

As a mom navigating my child's cancer journey, I can think back to some people who sat patiently with me. They prayed with me but did not pressure me to pray more. They accepted me as I was. They supported me. They said things such as, "Tina, I'm always here for you." They set their preconceived notions aside. In all of those ways, they showed me the kind of love that encourages healing.

We all want to experience expressions of empathy and to

know that someone truly cares for us, no matter what. We all want to be seen and heard as we are, without judgement. When we treat each other in this way, we are truly loving each other.

BEGIN INSIDE YOURSELF

My challenge to you is to start with yourself. We cannot extend love until we begin our own journey of healing by looking in the mirror to determine the messages we perceive, believe, and speak over ourselves. Whether we hold them consciously or subconsciously, the narratives that we live by as a result of unresolved wounds pose the risk of being projected onto other people. Our brokenness and unresolved pain create a level of deception that may cause blind spots and lead to continued hurt for ourselves and for the people God puts in our lives. We are to "take captive every thought to make it obedient to Christ" (2 Corinthians 10:5), renewing our minds (Romans 12:1–2). In this way, we will bring lasting change from the inside out.

Let the journey of love and healing begin in you. Seek to experience God's love in your heart so that you can share it with others. There is a story of hurt in the timeline of everyone's history. Out of His infinite love, Jesus set you free at the cross and redeemed you. You have only to receive what He has already done. He is not looking at you with judgement. His eyes are full of love, grace, and mercy.

It is Satan who wants to accuse you of your sins and trigger the wounds that cause you to stay behind your wall, because there you are unable to serve as a vessel of God's love who will help people to see their Saviour. Your true enemy is the accuser (Revelation 12:10–11), who seeks "to steal and kill and destroy," but Jesus has come so that you "may have life, and have it to the full" (John 10:10).

HELPING AND HEALING

I have worked with many people in various leadership positions over the course of my career. Once they felt safe in a place of empathy, where they knew that they were not being judged, stories of deep pain came to the surface. They were shocked at what was held in their souls and bodies, and they were finally able to experience healing in this environment of love. As we humbly spend time with people, genuinely caring for them, they will be able to release the wounds that have trapped them in harmful patterns and experience the true healing that brings lasting change.

Walking out our own stories with risk and vulnerability and learning to receive and experience the deep love of Jesus are among the greatest gifts we can give to another person. We cannot receive or give love authentically until we understand how our history has shaped our lives through wounds, walls, limitations, abilities, distractions, striving, and verbal and non-verbal communication.

Does this mean that you cannot help another person until you have addressed and released all your wounds? No, we do not have to wait to connect with other people until we have everything worked out for ourselves. Healing and sanctification are ongoing processes for all followers of Christ. We can journey in helping other people alongside our own healing journey. However, the more we open ourselves to self-awareness and introspection, the more we can help other people without being hindered by our own walls and wounds.

We are not called to be perfect. Perfection is not possible for anyone but Jesus Christ this side of heaven, and expecting it from ourselves and others leads only to further wounds. Instead, we are called to humble ourselves and point everyone to Jesus, who loves perfectly.

BEGIN TODAY

I encourage you to begin the process of your own healing today by creating a timeline of your life that lists positive and negative experiences. Map the positive experiences along the top of the horizontal timeline and the negative experiences along the bottom. Do not try to judge what is or is not essential. Just write.

Then sit in these experiences. Notice what your body tells you. Notice what your emotions tell you. Are you comfortable or uncomfortable? Do you feel calm and peaceful, or do you feel anxious or numb? What thoughts are revealed as you reflect on each of these experiences?

Our stories are not placed in nice, neat containers; they are compounded throughout our lives. They become stronger and stronger as our brains interpret experiences in ways that support the narratives we already hold in our souls.

164

I challenge you to take an honest look at yourself in the mirror. Do you see the eyes of Jesus' love, grace, and mercy looking at you, or do you see eyes of judgement, condemnation, and shame? Be willing, courageous, and vulnerable. The body of Christ needs leaders to stand authentically and imperfectly, revealing their wounds and walls, so they can show people the path to Jesus.

Chapter Ten Notes

_____

_____

_____

_____

_____

_____

_____

_____

_____

_____

_____

_____

_____

_____

_____

_____

_____

_____

_____

_____

_____

About the Author

Tina Smith is a Registered Social Worker and Psychotherapist, as well as a director, supervisor, teacher, and mentor. She is the founder of Tina J. Smith & Associates Counselling & Psychotherapy, a for-profit team of therapists that serves Christian and non-Christian individuals, couples, and families. Recently, Tina founded a not-for-profit charity called Selah Treatment Centre, of which she is executive director, to provide subsidized mental health healing and recovery. She is also the host of a radio program called *Rewired by Love*.

Tina is wife to Michael and mom to three children. They live in Woodstock, Ontario, Canada, with a Newfoundland named Atticus, a Havanese named Cuddles, and a cat named Cutie.

About Renown Publishing

Renown Publishing is the proud publishing imprint of Speak It To Book, an elite team of publishing professionals devoted to helping you shape, write, and share your book. Renown has written, edited, and worked on hundreds of books (including New York Times, Wall Street Journal, and USA Today best-sellers, and the #1 book on all of Amazon).

We believe authentic stories are the torch of change-makers, and our mission is to collaborate with purpose-driven authors to create societal impact and redeem culture.

If you're the founder of a purpose-driven company, visit RenownPublishing.com.

If you're an aspiring author, visit SpeakItToBook.com.

170

Notes

1. Lam, Vivian. "'We Know Very Little About the Brain': Experts Outline Challenges in Neuroscience." Scope. November 8, 2016. https://scopeblog.stanford.edu/2016/11/08/challenges-in-neuroscience-in-the-21st-century/.

Tompa, Rachel. "5 Unsolved Mysteries About the Brain." Allen Institute. March 14, 2019. https://alleninstitute.org/what-we-do/brain-science/news-press/articles/5-unsolved-mysteries-about-brain?gclid=EAIaIQobChMIlend6qud-wIVGsmUCR29NggqEAMYASAAEgI8LvD_BwE.

2. Zimmer, Carl. "100 Trillion Connections: New Efforts Probe and Map the Brain's Detailed Architecture." Scientific American. January 1, 2011. https://www.scientificamerican.com/article/100-trillion-connections/.

3. Demarin, V., S. Morović, and R. Béne. "Neuroplasticity." *Periodicum Biologorum* 116 (2014): p. 209–211.

4. Fuchs, Eberhard, and Gabriele Flügge. "Adult Neuroplasticity: More Than 40 Years of Research." *Neural Plasticity* (2014).

5. y Cajol, Santiago Ramon. *Recollections of My Life*. Translated by E. Horne Craigie and Juan Cano. Illustrated reprint edition. MIT Press, 1989.

6. Fuchs and Flügge, 2014.

7. Campbell, Celeste. "What Is Neuroplasticity?" Brainline. February 4, 2009. https://www.brainline.org/author/celeste-campbell/qa/what-neuroplasticity.

8. Lansing, Karen, Daniel G. Amen, Chris Hanks, and Lisa Rudy. "High-Resolution Brain SPECT Imaging and Eye Movement Desensitization and Reprocessing in Police Officers with PTSD. *Journal of Neuropsychiatry and Clinical Neurosciences* 17, no. 4 (2005): p. 526–532.

Rousseau, P. F., M. El Khoury Malhame, E. Reynaud, X. Zendjidjian, J. C. Samuelian, and S. Khalfa. "Neurobiological Correlates of EMDR Therapy Effect in PTSD." *European Journal of Trauma and Dissociation* 3 (2019): p. 103–111. http://estd.org/sites/default/files/files/1-s2.0-s2468749918300218-main.pdf.

9. "What Does 'Neurons That Fire Together Wire Together' Mean?" Super Camp. https://www.supercamp.com/what-does-neurons-that-fire-together-wire-together-mean.

10. Quoted in: Kresser, Chris. "RHR: Rewiring the Brain Through Neuroplasticity, with Dr. Caroline Leaf." Chris Kesser (website). March 3, 2021, https://chriskresser.com/rewiring-the-brain-through-neuroplasticity-with-dr-caroline-leaf/.

11. Leaf, Caroline. "Switch on Your Brain: The Key to Peak Happiness, Thinking, and Health." 2005.

Leaf, Caroline. "Our Brains Are Wired for Love." Q Ideas. December 3, 2021. YouTube video. https://www.youtube.com/watch?v=pTg6vbXkXKI.

12. Leaf, Caroline. "We Are Wired for Love." Living Word Christian Center. November 4, 2015. YouTube video. https://www.youtube.com/watch?v=Ds-S3fzJba4.

Roth, Sid. "Session III – Wired for Love ... Dr Caroline Leaf." TrueNorth Star. November 26, 2013. YouTube video. https://www.youtube.com/watch?v=m0DLRnaEAZk.

Believer's Voice of Victory. "Your Brain Is Wired for Love, Not Fear." Kenneth Copeland Ministries. June 14, 2018. YouTube video. https://www.youtube.com/watch?v=C8iiiKPccys.

Leaf, Caroline. *The Perfect You*. Baker Books, 2017.

13. Townsend, John. *Where Is God?* Thomas Nelson, 2009. Quoted in Kathy Brous, *Don't Try This Alone*. CreateSpace, 2018, p. 121.

14. Brous, Kathy. Preface to *Don't Try This Alone*. CreateSpace, 2018.

15. Findeisen, Barbara. *Womb Prints*. CreateSpace, 2017.

16. *Oxford Pocket Dictionary of Current English*, "mercy."

17. Brown, Brené. *The Gifts of Imperfection: Let Go of Who You Think You're Supposed to Be and Embrace Who You Are*. Hazelden, 2010.

18. Leaf, Caroline. "Through Her Eyes – the Sower and the Seed." Gatewaychurchtv. July 15, 2015. YouTube video. https://www.youtube.com/watch?v=YiXP_gBMPYs.

The Super Human Life Podcast. "Neuroscientist Explains How the Mind Is the Human Soul and Spirit w/ Dr. Caroline Leaf." April 13, 2021. https://www.youtube.com/watch?v=9jPXb9nnDuw.

19. van der Kolk, Bessel. *The Body Keeps the Score*. Penguin, 2014.

20. SickKids. "SickKids VS: MomStrong." April 10, 2017. YouTube video. https://www.youtube.com/watch?v=HvNF0yFUcx0.

21. Underwood, Carrie. "Jesus, Take the Wheel." Lyrics by Brett James, Hillary Lindsey, and Gordie Sampson. Track 4 on *Some Hearts*. Arista Nashville, 2005.

22. Brown, Brené. *Daring Greatly: How the Courage to Be Vulnerable Transforms the Way We Live, Love, Parent, and Lead*. Gotham, 2012.

23. Scazzero, Peter. *Emotionally Healthy Spirituality: Unleash a*

Revolution in Your Life in Christ. Thomas Nelson, 2006.

24. Shapiro, Francine. *Eye Movement Desensitization and Reprocessing (EMDR)*. EMDR Institute, 1995.

25. Keller, Timothy. *The Meaning of Marriage: Facing the Complexities of Commitment with the Wisdom of God*. John Murray Press, 2011.

26. Lifeway Research. "13 Stats on Mental Health and the Church." May 1, 2018. https://lifewayresearch.com/2018/05/01/13-stats-on-mental-health-and-the-church.

27. McConnell, Scott. Quoted in Lifeway Research, "Suicide Remains a Taboo Topic at Churches." September 29, 107. https://lifewayresearch.com/2017/09/29/suicide-remains-a-taboo-topic-at-churches.

28. Winell, Marlene. *Leaving the Fold: A Guide for Former Fundamentalists and Others Leaving Their Religion*. New Harbinger Publications, 1993.

29. Winell, Marlene. "Religious Trauma Syndrome." Journey Free: Recovery from Harmful Religion. July 13, 2016. https://www.journeyfree.org.

30. "What Is Religious Trauma?" Global Center for Religious Research. https://www.gcrr.org/religioustrauma.

31. Slade, Darren M. "No, Religious Trauma Is Not a 'Syndrome.'" Global Center for Religious Research. https://www.gcrr.org/post/religioustraumasyndrome-1.

32. Levine, Peter A. *Waking the Tiger: Healing Trauma*. North Atlantic Books, 1997, p. 128.

33. Finch, Jamie Lee. *You Are Your Own: A Reckoning with the Religious Trauma of Evangelical Christianity*. Amazon, 2019, p. 18.

34. Keller, *The Meaning of Marriage*.

35. Graham, Billy. "Truth Brings Freedom." Billy Graham Evangelistic Association. https://billygraham.org/devotion/truth-brings-freedom.

36. Wagner, Dee. "Polyvagal Theory in Practice." Counseling Today. June 27, 2016. https://ct.counseling.org/2016/06/polyvagal-theory-practice.

37. Brené, Brown. "The Power of Vulnerability." TEDx Houston. https://www.ted.com/talks/brene_brown_the_power_of_vulnerability/comments.

38. Gaither Vocal Band. "Let It Start in Me." *Sometimes It Takes a Mountain*. Gaither Music Group, 2014.

39. Brown, Brené. *Dare to Lead: Brave Work, Tough Conversations, Whole Hearts*. National Geographic Books, 2018, p. 10–11.

40. This anonymous quotation is widely circulated in discourse on trauma, emotional health, and related counseling.

41. Scazzero, Peter. *The Emotionally Healthy Leader: How Transforming Your Inner Life Will Deeply Transform Your Church, Team, and the World*. Zondervan, 2015, p. 25.

42. Branson-Potts, Hailey. "Another Young Pastor Advocating for Mental Health Dies by Suicide." Los Angeles Times. September 12, 2019. https://www.latimes.com/california/story/2019-09-12/california-megachurch-pastor-mental-health-suicide.

43. Perry, Bruce D., and Maia Szalavitz. *Born for Love: Why Empathy Is Essential—and Endangered*. Harper Collins, 2010, p. 5.

44. Perry and Szalavitz, *Born for Love*, p. 289.

45. Perry, Bruce D., and Maia Szalavitz. Introduction to *The Boy Who Was Raised as a Dog: And Other Stories from a Child Psychiatrist's Notebook*. Basic Books, 2007, p. xxvii.

46. Sharpley, Christopher F., Angela M. Jeffrey, and Terene McMah. "Counsellor Facial Expression and Client-Perceived Rapport." *Counselling Psychology Quarterly* 19, no. 4 (2006): p. 343–356.

Made in the USA
Middletown, DE
08 July 2023

34731319R00106